# Never Heave Your Bosom in a Front-Hook Bra

# *Modine Gunch*

## Created by Liz Scott

Illustrations by Rosemary Lewis

# Never Heave Your Bosom in a Front-Hook Bra

ST. MARTIN'S PRESS / NEW YORK

*Design by Amelia R. Mayone*

Library of Congress Cataloging-in-Publication Data

Gunch, Modine.
    Never heave your bosom in a front-hook bra / Modine Gunch.
      p.   cm.
    ISBN 0-312-04605-7
    I. Title.
  PN6162.G83   1990
  814'.54—dc20                       90-36137
                                       CIP

First Edition: October 1990
10 9 8 7 6 5 4 3 2 1

To the editors and staff, past and present, of *New Orleans Magazine*, who gave me encouragement and laughed at the right times. And to my husband, Art, and kids, who did the same.

# Contents

# Contents

# Creative Cleaning: Tips for Working Women

~~~~~~~~~~

Last night, my husband, Lout, is running late for his poker game. He gets out the shower and reaches for his underdrawers. There isn't any. "Modine!" he yells.

"Hold on," I say, thinking fast. "I got some drawers in the clean clothes pile."

There isn't a clean clothes pile, of course. It's a figment of my imagination. You work nine to five, and when do you have time to build up a clean clothes pile? I ask you that. Everybody in my house wears their stuff warm from the dryer. If they don't have time to wait for the dryer, they wear it wet.

So I grab some drawers from the dirty clothes hamper and sprinkle a little bleach on them and go out in the backyard and wave them around over my head a couple of times. By the time he's finished shaving, I am handing him his drawers, smelling all nice and fresh. What he don't know won't hurt him.

I call that creative. Most people, when they think about creative, they think about paintings and books and all. But the most creative people in the world are women who have to keep a house, a husband, kids, and a job—or any two of them—at the same time.

You got to be creative or you might as well slit your throat.

My mama used to mop floors with a mop and a bucket. I use a hose and towels tied to each foot. She cleaned the oven. I never cleaned the oven in twelve years, and it hasn't gotten no smaller.

She matched socks for everybody in the family. Everybody in this family wears the same color socks —light blue. They used to be white, but I washed them with a pair of new blue jeans once.

If I forget to put the chicken out to defrost, I just run it through the dishwasher. Without soap, naturally.

One of the times when I was pregnant, I run out of undies myself. So I just reach in Lout's drawer and grab a pair of his. I look like a barn with feet when I'm pregnant, but so what. Lout is not exactly a light-weight. The pants fit, so I wear 'em . . .

All the way to work I worry about getting in an accident. You know how your grandmother always warns you not to go out in panties with holes in them because if you get in an accident and don't get killed, everybody at the hospital will talk and you will be embarrassed for the rest of your life? I think about this, and I think about what the hospital people will say if they see me in a pair of Lout's drawers.

Well, I don't get in an accident, but I do forget I have them on, and I stop in a maternity shop on the way home. To try on a cute little maternity top I see in the window. Wouldn't you know, the saleslady is one of those nosy kind. When I am changing, she says, "Is everything okay, Honey?" and yanks open the curtain. You should see the expression on her face. I guess she thinks I am a morphodite or something.

But it serves her right. She don't understand. Working women have got to be creative these days.

# Emergency Plans for Piece Meal Thanksgiving

~~~~~~~~~~

Back in olden times, like you read about in the Bible, when people want to give thanks for something, what they do is, they cast a virgin in a volcano. (It was very dangerous to be a old maid back then.) Or they slay a fatted ox or a innocent lamb and throw that in the volcano.

Which makes sense. I'd a lot rather slay a fatted ox than cook a turkey. My luck with turkeys ain't so great. One Thanksgiving, a couple of years ago, I think I'll save a lot of trouble by cooking the turkey in a plastic bag. My husband, Lout, says that instead of wasting money on one of those special baking bags that comes in the little box with directions and all, why not use a big black garbage bag I have lying around? (It don't have garbage in it, of course.) I don't like to talk about how that turns out. You know blackened redfish? That is supposed to be good, but turkey in melted black plastic is not good. Remember that.

Sometimes I wish I could slay Lout and cast him in a volcano.

And then there is last year. Like every other year, Lout's mama, Larda Gunch, and his big brother, Leech, and his little brother, Lurch, are coming over.

Anyway, the night before, I put the turkey out on the back steps to defrost. Next morning, I preheat the oven and go out to get my turkey. It is gone.

I yell for the kids, of course, and of course they look at me with their mouths hanging open to show how innocent they are. My daughter Gumdrop says probably a cat got it. That makes me stop and think. If there is a cat around that can eat a twenty-two pound turkey, I guess I better keep an eye on the baby.

Then Lout comes out of the bathroom. He gropes around for his coffee, and once he gets it and focuses his eyes, he says, "You need to be more careful, Modine. I almost broke my neck coming in last night. I tripped over a turkey you had left out on the back steps." Then, he goes on, real proud of himself, he put it back in the freezer where it belonged. I looked, and it was in there, all right—hard as a rock. I couldn't defrost that before dinner if I used a blowtorch.

I think about the volcano again. Then I start thinking, maybe, if I get enough beer in the Gunches, they won't know a turkey from a Whopper. But my mama-in-law always brings oyster dressing, and I'll need to put it in something.

So I run to the supermarket, which is, thank God,

open. Of course, they don't have any turkeys left. But after I whine and moan and carry on a while, the butcher remembers they have some turkey pieces in the back. Not whole turkeys though, just cut-up pieces. I am thinking about sticking them together with the oyster dressing, to make a whole turkey, but what they have is three drumsticks, two necks, three wings, and a couple of breasts. The breasts are smoked, but I don't notice that. I take them home.

I am a little nervous, of course. The Gunches come in wearing their stretch pants, which means they are counting on some serious eating. I peel a potato and add some pieces of potato peel to the powdered mashed potato to give it a nice authentic touch. I get rid of the wrappers from the pecan pies and sprinkle a couple of nutshells in them. I add some 7-Up to the Ripple to make it sparkle more and last longer. And I stick the turkey parts in the oven, shoving the oyster dressing on top of the breasts. Bringing oyster dressing is a tradition with Lout's mama. She's done it every year since the first year I cooked a turkey and stuffed it with half a loaf of sandwich bread. I thought that was what bread stuffing meant.

When the turkey parts are cooked, I call Lout in, and he pretends he is cutting up the turkey in the kitchen. "Ooh, man," he says through the door. "Dis is a lot of work. Bring me the electric knife. Bring me the meat cleaver. Bring me a ax."

When my mother-in-law says we ought to bring the whole turkey to the table, I tell her the turkey platter is under the air-conditioner catching the drips, which is true.

So we swing the TV set around to face the table, and we say our grace during the first commercial, and we all start shoveling it in. Between watching the TV and watching their own plates to make sure nothing gets away, the Gunches don't notice that this turkey has three necks. But after a while Leech looks up and says, "These are pretty weird breasts." I sit up straight and glare at him, and I say, "Don't talk dirty on Thanksgiving!" That shuts him up, and we finish eating.

Then I get rid of the paper plates and bring out toothpicks, and we all sit around for a couple of hours and belch. It was a pretty nice Thanksgiving after all.

# Wear Red and Green, and Smile Fast for a Picture Poifect Christmas

That song that starts "Christmas is comin' and the goose is getting fat" always makes me think about my husband, Lout. Nobody loves Christmas more than Lout. Not that he's the sentimental type. But Christmas always involves food, which he also loves.

Nothing in the kitchen is ever safe from Lout. One year I got one of those potpourris. The directions said to boil it in water to make the house smell festive. So I do. But Lout sees it there, bubbling on the stove, and he drinks it. I don't know if it would have worked for the house, but Lout don't smell too festive.

So I always got to be careful. Like, if I have to save a specimen for the doctor, I never keep it in my refrigerator. I got to use my neighbor Awlette's refrigerator. Better her husband make a mistake than mine.

We used to have a Christmas tradition where Lout would go out and cut down the tree with his very own hands. Until the people from the church down the street pass by and tell me, in a very mean way, that the pine trees that grow on each side of their walkway, that they paid a landscape artist good money to put there, were disappearing at the rate of one a year. So now we get a artificial tree.

But everybody thinks it's natural because the whole house smells like a big Christmas tree. I know how to do that, without potpourri, and without leaving a bottle of Pine-Sol open, like Lout wants to do. I just rake up some pine needles and drop them down the floor furnace. Then the house smells Christmasy right through Mardi Gras.

Last year, Lout's mama, Miss Larda, decides we should have a family picture taken to send around on Christmas cards. Lout's brother Leech borrows one of those cameras that you set up on a little tripod, and you have ten seconds to run in front of it and it takes your picture.

Lout wants us all to pose in front of a fireplace, but none of us have a fireplace. I say we should take it with us all standing on the floor furnace because that is where we stand all winter anyway. If there is anything that feels as good on a cold, wet day as standing on a hot floor furnace, I don't know what it is. I feel sorry for people with central heat. Awlette's house

is like that, and she says sometimes she just takes her hair dryer and aims it down her back. But I bet it's not the same.

Anyway, Lout's other brother, Lurch, has a new

second-hand Mustang convertible, which is red. He says if we all sit in it and wear green, the picture will be in Christmas colors.

So we all get dressed in green, except Lout, who dresses up in his Santa Claus suit. He loves it because he don't have to suck in his stomach to wear it. One of his boots is gone. I don't say nothing. I never did figure out how my baby daughter Gladiola got it over the edge of the toilet. So Lout just wears his flip-flops. Leech shows up in a shirt that is green all right, but it has "Kiss Me, I'm Irish" on it and a big pair of red lips. He says the colors are right.

So he sets up the camera for thirty seconds and we all smile like crazy and jump in the car at the same time. The kids, being fastest, get in first, which turns out to be a mistake. Because everybody else jumps in on top of them, of course. I thought we would have to revive Gumdrop, and my son Gargoyle gets knocked out of his little green tennis shoes like people do when they are hit by a train.

So we finally all just stand in front of the car and pose. When the picture comes out, Gargoyle has his finger in his nose. And after all that green business, it turns out that Leech's friend has black and white film in the camera. Anyway, I make a bunch of copies in a copying machine, and underneath I write "Merry" in red marker and "Christmas" in green. Merry Christmas to you too.

# Sweat and Dance Lead
# to Sweet Romance

~~~~~~~

My sister-in-law, Larva, is over at my house crying and carrying on. She says she has got a negative body image. I don't know about that, but I do know she got a body image she can't see in the mirror all at one time. Larva weighs around three hundred pounds, butt naked. And she is in love.

The object of her affections is named Mayer the Slayer. He is the roach man who sprays her house. She has even painted him a T-shirt—Mayer the Slayer and a heart with a arrow in gold. But he finally tells her right out that he is not about to be turned on by anybody who is twice as big as him. I can understand that. I myself have to sleep with one arm clenched over the side of the mattress, to keep from rolling over onto my husband Lout's side of the bed. Lout has got a body image even bigger than Larva's, and his side is sunk about three feet lower than my side.

Anyway, while Larva is pouring out her heart, Lout barges in. He gets his virtuous look on and tells her that she ought to exercise a lot, like him.

That chokes her up in mid-sob, and I ask him what he's talking about, exercise. He says, with his mouth all pursed up, that did I forget he goes bowling every single Thursday night? Larva tells him bowling is no good, and she is going to join a ladies' figure salon. He says he can bowl off forty pounds before she can sweat it off at no figure salon. So they make a bet, and the loser is supposed to treat the winner to all the crawfish they can eat. Plus beer.

So the next day, Larva and myself go check out this figure salon. It seems like a combination between Santa Claus's workshop and hell. All these women busy working—each at a different kind of torture machine. One pushes their legs apart while they try to close them. Another holds their ankles up in the air, and they try to pull them down.

Everybody is all got up like ballet dancers in leotards and tights. Some of them have figures like ballet dancers, but a lot have figures like myself and Larva and even worse.

We join a aerobic dance class, where you jump and prance around and do high kicks for a long time without stopping. I have borrowed my daughter Gumdrop's tights, which is a mistake. The crotch is two or three inches below my crotch. So it is a real fight to do the high kicks. And the dance instructor must have used to have been a drill sergeant in the Marines because she keeps yelling stuff like, "Are we happy?"

and if we don't yell back, "Yah, we happy!" she sings out, "I can't hearrr you." Me, I can think of things I'd rather yell.

Larva is doing all this in a plastic sweatsuit. Afterwards, it is stuck to her, and I wind up cutting it off, like you cut silver paper off a baked potato. Only Larva don't smell like no baked potato, poor thing.

Once is enough for me but Larva keeps going every day. And she starts shrinking.

Lout gets nervous. He is beginning to think he is going to have to buy her the crawfish dinner, and that is going to mean a ugly death for a lot of crawfish. Also for his poker money.

So one evening he sneaks over to the salon to see what is going on in there. He don't go in because in a leotard he would look conspicuous. He just stands by the window and looks in.

When he gets home his face is red, and he's breathing funny. I think he's having a heart attack. I get him a glass of water.

"I never seen anything like it. All them butts. Rows and rows of butts, wiggling and jiggling and bouncing. And thighs! Thighs going in, thighs going out . . ." I just throw the water on him. I don't need to hear filthy talk.

But Larva, she keeps shrinking, and pretty soon The Slayer is acting very interested. But it's too late. She is after bigger game now.

So, to tell you the happy ending, Larva marries a stock boy at Schwegmann's who is also a Japanese Sumo wrestler. His name is Fred. And they move to Japan. I think Larva feels like Madame Butterfly now. Ain't that cute?

# A Woman Has to Look
# Out for Number One

If I want my legs to look hairy, I can just stop shaving them. I sure don't got to go pay good money for pantyhose with little squiggly things all over them.

My neighbor Awlette, she buys those kind—textured. Only blue ones. She says her varicose veins meld right in with the lace and don't hardly show up at all. Now that makes sense. But it only works if you got veins the right shade of blue.

Even just plain pantyhose can mean trouble. Like when you yank on a pair in a hurry, and you are halfway where you're going before you realize that they are too small. The crotch is not in your crotch. It is on its way to your knees.

So you start slinking along, walking like a cat does when it rubs against somebody's legs, thinking you can make the crotch work itself back up. It don't work.

So you get behind something, like the bus stop shelter, look around to make sure nobody is looking, and real fast swat yourself between the legs a few times. It don't work. And then you notice somebody *is* looking, and God knows what they think.

So you decide just to put up with it and go along like a duck, just walking from the knees down, but you know they are going to keep on slipping, and pretty soon you'll only be able to walk from the ankles down. Pretty soon you can't stand it any more.

This time you make sure you're alone, then quick slip your hand under your clothes and grab the elastic waistband and pull up. You jump and dance around a little bit, pulling hard. Then the pantyhose rips.

Sometimes I think women are our own worst enemies. We are love slaves to fashion.

Now everything's big. Big shirts, baggy pants. Sure, it feels good. You can shove all your fat in there and nobody sees it. But after everybody has let go and been eating everything in sight and gets their baggy clothes to almost fit, what's going to happen? You know what's going to happen. Tight clothes are gonna come back in style. And everybody will be trying to squish their big buns into little bitty pants that fit like pantyhose. Like trying to shove a bag of marshmallows into a rubber glove. Girdle makers are going to have a field day. Sometimes I wonder if we aren't stupid.

I don't know how long it took them to invent clothes that you don't have to iron, but they finally did it. And what happens? Everybody starts carrying

on about how they got to have natural fabrics that breathe.

My daughter Gumdrop never seen an iron until she was twelve. Nobody even told her to roll all the laundry up and put it in the freezer and iron it when she felt like it, like my mama told me to do when I was first married to Lout. I did it, too. Of course, I never did feel like ironing. Pretty soon you couldn't even fit a Popsicle in there.

Lout didn't care. He says nothing feels as good as a cold shirt on a hot day. He still keeps his drawers in there in the summer.

But now, Gumdrop and my son, Gargoyle, all they want is natural, natural, natural. Natural means it looks like you slept in it. Forget washing machines. Natural means you gotta wash it every other Tuesday when the moon is full. By hand. With natural soap. And let it drip naturally dry over the tub. And when your daddy tries to take a bath he yells out some pretty unnatural things.

Still and all, last week Lout buys himself a 100-percent cotton shirt. Probably they had to use up a whole field of cotton to make a shirt his size. A circus elephant could get comfortable in one of Lout's shirts.

Anyway, here's Lout in his false hairpiece, with his four false teeth, walking around saying his shirt is natural. So natural I am supposed to iron it.

Luckily, Lout forgets that cotton shrinks in warm water. I boil it a while before I wash it. I tell Lout that natural stuff has to be sterilized. When I finish with it, it would of fit a Cabbage Patch Doll.

So much for natural. So much for ironing. A woman has to look out for number one.

# Sequins, Satins, and Roach Suits—Let the Big Mothuhs Roll!

~~~~~

L et the good times roll. They were talking about truck floats when they made that saying up.

We belong to the Big Mothuhs Carnival Club and this year we made a float that is absolutely gorgeous. It is called Spray for Me, and the theme is Roaches of New Orleans. Our truck bathroom is made to look like a can of bug spray, and every two and a half minutes a puff of smoke comes out of the nozzle. It is coming from a pan of dry ice behind the nozzle, not from anything that is being done in the bathroom.

Everybody who rides is dressed like different roaches. It is very educational. The larger persons are dressed like the big roaches that the roach man always tells you come in your house from outside, but don't breed in there. They are dark brown. The smaller persons, like me, are indoor roaches, and we dress in a lighter brown. And the kids dress like roach eggs, and they wear maroon. A member of our club who is a roach man himself, Bubba Mayer—also known as Mayer the Slayer—he is a couturier in his spare time, and he designed the costumes.

The people in our club got a passion for sequins. They got a love affair going with sequins. The more sequins on a costume, the better, they think. The sequins are gonna dazzle the judges, they say. They add another 4,800 sequins to the 2,032 sequins Bubba already designed on the costume.

Each roach has four bands across his stomach, made of gold sequins. He has a face outlined in maroon sequins. He has clusters of silver sequins at the tips of his antennas, and again at each of his six little hands that are attached by springs to the sides of his costume.

But these creative geniuses don't got to put on the sequins. This year, *I* got to put on 68,320 of them.

Usually Lout's mama, Miss Larda, does this. She is real good with her hands. Once she even made a outfit for herself out of the couch slipcover, just like Scarlett O'Hara did out of the drapes. Every year she sits down and runs up the costumes for me and Lout, for herself and Lout's brothers Leech and Lurch, his sister Larva and her husband Fred, and my kids, Gumdrop, Gargoyle, and little Gladiola. Ten costumes.

But this year, fate steps in. Miss Larda reads in the papers about a special on chickens at Schwegmann's. (It's tradition—you got to take fried chicken for a truck ride and throw a bone off the side every once in a while along with the beads.) So she rushes

over, and she is hurrying to the meat counter, when she slips on a grape in the aisle. She slides through the stacked-up boxes of bran flakes and ends up in the ground meat special, which cushions her landing.

It could of happened to anybody. But she twists her arm and she can't sew.

So I'm elected. She brings over seventy yards of carnival satin and three bolts of sequins and leaves me alone with them. I have to turn them into prizewinning roach suits. I feel like that girl in *Rumplestiltskin*.

I make costumes for Halloween all right, vampires and bats and ghosts, but they can't take the light of day. This is because I make them out of Hefty bags and staples. But I never made ten roaches with sequins.

I read the directions on the patterns. I can't understand them. I notice that they are repeated in Spanish and French. I feel like the pattern company is being sarcastic. If I can't understand them in English, how am I going to understand them in Spanish and French?

I call up my neighbor Awlette, who, thank God, knows about sewing. She comes over with her machine, and between the two of us, and Gumdrop with a stapler and Gargoyle with the Quik glue, we get them all put together by midnight before Mardi Gras. Lout grouches because his bands run up and down instead of sideways (I tell him they are slenderizing that way), and Leech is missing a few legs, and we switched the leg and waist measurements of Gargoyle's so his pants look like they are made for a very fat dwarf. But so what? It's Mardi Gras. And we roll, and we have a good time.

# Bosom Betrayal:
# Women Versus Bras

It's got to be men who design bras. Maybe one man. A sadist. My mother-in law, Larda Gunch, and me were talking about it.

My mother-in-law knows plenty about bras. She is the hefty type, and she got a figure like a wedge. She says she'd been a D cup since the day she was born.

Anyway, this sadist eventually thought about inventing bras that close in the front, she says.

"It sounds like such a tremendous idea, Modine," she says to me. "Everybody has trouble getting bras open when the hook is in the back. One time, I spend a half a hour trying to get one off so I can take a shower. Finally, I give up and try to pull it off over my head.

I get stuck with half of me in and half of me out, and the doorbell rings and I almost strangle myself trying to get the rest of it off. I never do find out who is at the door.

"So when these kind that fasten in front came out, we all run out and buy them. But sooner or later the same thing happens to everybody. And it always happens when you're in a bus or a elevator or something."

I know what happens. I am in the checkout line at Schwegmann's when it happens to me. And it is worse because I wear a padded bra. All of a sudden the thing snaps open—click—and the elastic band across the back immediately yanks the two cups apart, zip, and I am standing there looking like I have breasts in my armpits.

This same man who designed the bras probably also figured out how to hang them in the stores. Ever notice how they hang up bras? They have them all on this wall, arranged by size. So far this makes sense. But then, they put the smallest cup sizes, the teeny weeny triple A's and them, up at the top of the wall. And the big old D and E cups are down at the bottom. This means that little bitty girls like my daughter Gumdrop are hopping up and down trying to snatch their tiny bras off the rack, and the bigger, older ladies like Larda are crawling along the floor, huffing and puffing, rooting around for their size.

It's a man's world, all right. Excuse me for bringing up a delicate subject, but I bet they don't arrange athletic supporters like that. How do they size those things, anyway? Does anybody go in a store and ask for a double A or a great big E? I am afraid to ask.

I remember when Gumdrop made up her mind

to get a training bra. At that time, she don't have nothing to train. She don't even have warts on her ribs.

But she says all the girls in the sixth grade wear

a bra. You can tell, she says, because she is in Catholic school, and they all have to wear white blouses. When they lean forward in their desks, you can see the wide elastic bands across their backs. That means they have bras. Everybody but her. I tell her to wrap a Ace bandage around her chest. It would fit better.

But Gumdrop is her daddy's little sweetie pie. If Gumdrop wants something, Gumdrop knows who to go whining to. And she whines up a storm. "How much can one of them things cost?" Lout finally grumps. "It's worth it to shut her up."

I will say this for Lout. When he makes up his mind, he is a man of action.

So he walks into J. C. Penney's, right into the lingerie section. (Actually it takes him a while because he don't know "lingerie" means the same thing as underwear.) But he finds it, and he goes up to the counter, and he stands there, all three hundred pounds of him, and he says, "I want a training bra."

The lady gets out a little stretchy thing labeled "one size fits all." And she points to the label and says, "Sir, I don't think that this is true in *all* cases." Lout don't realize she thinks the bra is for him. He just says, "Well, if it don't fit I'll bring it back." I bet the lady was on the phone telling her husband *that* one the minute Lout was out of sight.

Anyway, when Gumdrop gets it she jumps up and down and squeals and runs off and puts it on with a white blouse to make sure you can see the band through the back. She is so happy. Poor heart. She's got a long road ahead.

# A Mother's Day Moral:
# Look Before You Leap,
# or Every Saint
# Has His Day

W hat do you get on Mother's Day if you have
kids? You know what. A card with flowers
that are made out of pink toilet paper—a
lot of pink toilet paper. You get breakfast in bed. Then
you get up and fix everybody else their breakfast. And
then you go to the bathroom, and you are out of toilet
paper. Which is a blessing in a way because, while
you are sitting there, you have time to reflect about
what it's going to be like when the kids are grown up
and gone. Maybe they'll at least leave the toilet paper
be.

My husband Lout's mama, Miss Larda, thinks
she is getting support hose in rainbow colors like usual,

but I am going to surprise her with a bunch of chocolate roses. But I'll have to wrap them up in silver paper and hide them in the freezer and tell Lout they are a pork butt, or she will wind up with naked stems.

My mother-in-law never asks for candy for a present. She says she spent too many years getting two-pound boxes of chocolates with five pieces in them, all spaced out to look like that was all there was in the box in the first place. All her kids got a uncontrollable passion for chocolate. She should of given them names like Milk Dud and Snickers and Goo Goo Cluster, instead of Lout, Leech, Larva, and Lurch.

A lot of people ask her why she picked names that all started with L. Well, the reason is that my mother-in-law is a woman with a interesting past. When she had the kids, she was married to a Italian boy, whose last name started with L. She thought the initials L.L. would be classy. Her husband was a Lollapaloosa. And from what I understand, Mr. Lollapaloosa had a roving eye. Other parts of him roved too, but Miss Larda loved him anyway. He got real sick one day—just went into a decline—and it seemed like he would die and Larda would be left with all them little mouths to feed. And them little mouths wanted to be fed a lot. It must have been like keeping a pack of St. Bernards around the house.

If Miss Larda is anything, it is religious. She got right down on her knees and started a flying novena to St. Jude. A regular novena is when you pray every night for nine days, or once a week for nine weeks. With a flying novena, you set the alarm clock, and you

drop down on your knees every half hour and get all
the praying done in one day.

The first time I saw Miss Larda do this, I thought

she was having a heart attack. The alarm would go
off, she would plunk down wherever she was and shut
her eyes to concentrate and roar out the prayers, real
fast. Then she would get up and drip herself a cup of

coffee and drink it. Then she would go to the bathroom, because of the coffee I guess. By then the alarm would go off and the whole thing would start over again.

When St. Joseph's Day came around, she decided to get him in the act. She got a bunch of friends together to make food for a St. Joseph's altar. This is a big altar, two or three tiers, covered with food. You set it up on St. Joseph's Day, and at the end of the day, you give it all away. So they got everything set up, and it was gorgeous. But that same morning, wouldn't you know, Mr. Lollapaloosa dropped dead. He had been getting better and sneaked off to see this girl named Bimbette. Well, Bimbette's husband came home unexpected, and Mr. Lollapaloosa leaped for the bedroom locker to hide, but he miscalculated and leaped through Bimbette's French windows instead. The balcony didn't hold, so he dropped three stories, and that was that.

Poor Miss Larda had no choice but to eat all the St. Joseph's altar food herself. She said St. Joseph hadn't kept up his end of the deal. She gave him his chance.

But St. Joseph showed her. On that very day a year later, she married Gomer Gunch. Gomer Gunch was a bricklayer. And he worked for—get this—the St. Joe Brick Works. Don't that make the hair on the back of your neck stand up? So all the kids changed their last names to Gunch because it's easier to spell. My husband, he says he'll always be thankful to St. Joseph for that.

# Fear of Flying? Grab Your Ankles and Don't Flush Over Big Cities

If I ever win a million dollars and get rich, I am not joining the jet set, I can tell you that. And it's not just because they are always snorting their Cokes and doing other disgusting things. It is because I would be too terrified to jet. If I had to get back and forth from some Greek island to the Himalayas every week, I would take the bus.

Because if a bus breaks down, it just goes over to the side of the road, and you can get out and be mad until another bus comes along. But if a plane breaks down, it *goes* down. I think about that a lot.

I think about it especially when my husband, Lout, wins the Cat Lovers Getaway for Two to Acapulco for sending in the label off a can of cat food.

(We don't have a cat—much less love one. I thought that was a can of tuna fish when I bought it, and Lout thought it was tuna fish when he ate it. I should of known nothing good would come from that.)

Lout is real excited when he finds out he won. "When are we going to have another chance like this, Modine?" he says. "When are we going to have another chance to plunge into the desert in a ball of flames?" I say. But Lout ignores that and calls up the travel agency. He gets the name of the airline and the time and all, and he don't even ask whether this airline has ever succesfully flown a plane to Mexico before, or whether their planes generally stay up in the air or anything. I mean, you got to say it politely, but there are some things you should ask.

I know I got to go with him. I don't want him getting any ideas about maybe asking Maybelline from the bowling alley where he works. So I go out and get a new bathing suit and some gold toenail polish, and I try to act real cheerful.

My friend Awlette passes by to give me some advice. When she was a little girl, she went on the train a lot to visit her grandma in Dry Prong.

"You got to be real careful about using the bathroom," she says. "I remember from the train, that if you looked in the toilet when you flushed it, you could see the ground rushing by. So on the plane, if you got to go, at least don't go when you're over any big cities. Have a little consideration."

She also says to watch the papers. "Hope for a couple of big plane crashes just before you leave," she says. "That way, odds are, there won't be another one for a while." She learned to think like that from playing the horses.

My mother-in-law, Miss Larda, she also feels jumpy about airplanes, but she tries to be very subtle about it. "Did you and Lout get those burial plots paid off, Modine?" she says. "Under some circumstances, you know, people don't need their plots after all, like when for some reason or other there ain't any remains to speak of."

She also cuts out a article from the papers where a expert is telling how to survive a plane crash. I don't know how come he's such a expert. It don't say how many crashes he has survived that makes him a expert, but you'd think by now he'd take the bus.

He says sit in a aisle seat next to the rearmost overwing exit, and if you "sense anything wrong, get into the brace position of head down and ankles grabbed without waiting for an attendant to tell you." Suppose you sense something wrong and there isn't anything wrong? There you are, bent over, staring into your crotch. But the other people on the plane aren't staring into their crotches. They are probably staring at you. Would you ever have the nerve to sit up and show your face again? You might as well just hang onto your ankles for the whole trip.

Anyway, the big day finally comes and the whole family comes to see us off. As we are going through the X-ray machine, smiling and waving, my son, Gargoyle, yells out, "JUST HOPE THE PLANE DON'T CRASH!" He never was the subtle type.

When the lady asks smoking or nonsmoking, I say, "Rearmost overwing exit, please." She looks at us funny, but that is where we sit. And wouldn't you know, the plane don't crash. So I am glad I never grabbed my ankles.

# Coffee, Snakes, and Pantyhose: Highway Hazards for the Absentminded

You keep hearing about all these sensitive men who eat quiche and all. My husband, Lout, eats quiche because he never says no to anything that's food, but that don't mean anything.

For instance, we are taking a ride the other day, and this lady drives past, dressed up nice and smiling to herself. But right over her head, on the roof of the car, is a book. Its pages are flapping in the air, and it looks like it is getting ready to fall off any minute. Lout says, "Will you look at that idiot. Carries her book on top the car."

Now, if *sensitive* has a opposite, that's it. Most people know right away that the poor thing just went outside with stuff in both hands and set the book on the car roof while she got her keys out. And then she forgot about it. We know it because we do it too.

One time, I myself set a Styrofoam cup of coffee up there, and I just drive off. It tilts over, and the coffee runs down the windshield and I think it is raining, and I turn the windshield wipers on. Then I notice the drops are brown, so I start getting worried, wondering if it is some of that acid rain. At the next red light, I stick my head out the window to look at the sky, and the cup falls on my head. So I think, "That's what we get for fooling around with rockets—things falling right out of the sky." After a while I realize what it is, and I just drive off like nothing happened and ignore the people who started to gather around when I jumped out the car and screamed a little bit about the Russians. It could happen to anybody.

Now Lout claims he has never been absent-minded in his life. But he causes enough trouble anyway. One time he sees a snake in a tree in front of our house. Anybody else would let well enough alone and hope the snake just stays there, or else go and get a BB gun and shoot it. Not Lout. He is gonna capture it alive and sell it to the pet shop for money.

So he pokes at it with a stick, and the stick is too short. His mama's car is nearby, so he pushes it a few feet until it is under the tree and he climbs up on it. He still can't reach the snake, so he goes inside to get a butterfly net or something. While he is gone, the snake decides to hell with it and drops down on the car roof. But before Lout comes back, his mama, Miss Larda, comes and gets in the car and starts off.

The snake must not like the feeling of the wind because it starts to slither down across the windshield in front of her face. Miss Larda, she forgets that there is glass between her and the snake, and all she can think of is scrape the snake off, which she does by driving through the big hedge in my friend Awlette's yard. She stops the car under the clothesline and wiggles out through the sun roof, encounters a pair of Awlette's good black pantyhose (which, I guess, look like a snake if you are hysterical) and pounds them right into the ground. It turns out okay though. Miss Larda pays Awlette back for the pantyhose, and Lout pays for the hedge.

And I remember our trip to Florida. About halfway there, Lout decides that there is too much wind in the car, so he cranks up his window and then he reaches back without looking around and cranks up the window behind him. What he don't bother to notice is that our son, Gargoyle, has got his head stuck out that window.

The kids are making so much racket we don't hear Gargoyle's yells, which are muffled because his mouth is now outside with the rest of his face. Gargoyle's sisters, quite naturally, don't tell us anything. People driving by honk and scream and point but Lout just says, "Look at them maniacs."

Finally I notice that Gargoyle don't grab like usual when I get out the cookie bag, and I look around and see what happened. Gargoyle don't seem no worse for wear when we get the rest of him back in the car, except for a few smashed bugs on his ears, but I am very upset just the same. Lout says it is Gargoyle's fault for having his head out in the first place. "Other people are absentminded," he insists, "but I don't make no mistakes I don't intend to." I think about that a lot.

# Add to the List of Lent

I ask my son, Gargoyle, what he's giving up for Lent and he tells me socks. What can I say to that?

I guess I should count my blessings and not argue with less laundry. But if he gives up drawers I will put my foot down. Going around without drawers is probably a sin.

Anyway, I thank God for Lent. After we stuff our faces from Thanksgiving through Mardi Gras, we need it. Otherwise, people would be exploding in the streets.

Besides, giving up something for Lent is better than giving it up for New Year's. Lent only lasts forty days. And you get time off in purgatory for giving it up. If you make a New Year's resolution, you got to quit for at least a year, and you get no Brownie points in the next life.

My husband Lout's family, they kill two birds with one stone every year. They always give up everything that will make them fatter. Last year my mother-in-law, Miss Larda, she gives up beer, sweets, and all starches except garlic bread. (She says there are two things life isn't worth living without. One of them is "The Golden Girls" and the other one is garlic bread.)

Lout outdoes her and gives up garlic bread too. He makes his list as big as possible. Then he spends the rest of the forty days trying to think of something he left off the list so he can eat it. One year it is ketchup and raisins. They don't fall into any of the other categories, he says. They aren't starch and they aren't sweet. So he eats a lot of them. It's hard to eat ketchup all by itself, but he don't mind dipping the raisins in it, like they are little bitty French fries. I lose a few pounds myself just from disgust watching him.

Anyway, in Lent there are a lot of exceptions to make things easier. A regular diet is usually seven days a week, twenty-four hours a day. You can get fat any minute, any second, any hour. But in Lent, you don't have to count the Sundays. So people like Lout and his family stay up late, watching the clock on Saturday nights. On the stroke of midnight, they tear the refrigerator door off and eat a twenty-four hour meal. All this don't count, though, because it's Sunday. Also St. Patrick's Day don't count (God can't make you fat on St. Patrick's Day), and St. Joseph's Day don't count, of course, and if St. Valentine's Day falls during Lent, that don't count either.

This year, Lout decides he is going to give up food altogether during Lent except for days that don't count, of course. He is going to go on a liquid diet.

So he buys this protein powder, which, he figures, if you throw a few bananas into it, won't taste too bad.

You mix it up in a blender into a kind of milkshake. He tells me he is going to be saving me a lot of work cooking for him. Just give him his protein milkshake three times a day.

And he sticks to it for a while. Of course, I could make a fortune if I charge a admission fee at feeding time. You never saw a blender full of anything go down anybody so fast.

I decide to make it real, real thick so it will take

longer to get it down. Miss Larda tells me she learned at Weight Watchers how to do this without adding any calories. You just add lots of ice cubes. You drop them in one at a time while the blender is going. My blender has this cover with a clear plastic center shaped like a knob you can lift out, so you can drop the ice cubes in without taking the whole cover off and getting yourself splashed with what you are mixing up.

It works real nice for two days. But on the third day I am in a hurry, trying to cook for the kids and fix Lout his swill at the same time. I slap the lid on without looking and I slap it on upside down and the clear plastic center falls into the liquid part. I don't notice this. I just drop all the ice cubes in and give it to Lout. I notice he crunches a little, but he don't complain. After supper Gumdrop decides to use the blender to make herself a real shake with ice cream and all. By this time I am just figuring out what happened. She says, "What happened to the blender lid?" and I say, real low, "Daddy ate it."

Wouldn't you know, Lout hears me. You never heard such a yowl. I think he is going to want to be rushed to the hospital, but instead he rushes to the refrigerator. "Who knows how many calories was in that lid?" he roars. "Probably thousands. There's no sense trying any more. You just blew my whole diet." And he proceeds to blow it some more. So much for Lent. So much for time off purgatory. He says if it wasn't for me, he'd be a thin man by now. And would one day probably be canonized a saint. But I doubt it.

# How Many Times
# Can a Nudist Sin?

Now, don't go thinking I got a filthy mind, but I bet nudists save a lot of money. They don't spend it on clothes. That's obvious. If the hemlines go up, what do they care? Their hemlines are already up. They don't got to buy laundry detergent. Or bleach. They never set foot inside a washateria. Or a Singer sewing machine shop. Or even learn to thread a needle. They must have so much money and spare time they don't know what to do with theirselves.

Don't get me wrong. I was brought up religious, and I know it's got to be a mortal sin to run around stark naked. Probably it is a lot of mortal sins. Probably it is a mortal sin every time they get up and don't get dressed in the morning. And another mortal sin every time they take a shower and prance out with no bathrobe on. Nudists must have souls blacker than the suntans they probably also have.

So I am not going to run off and join the nudists, yet. But I think about it a lot. Which is also probably a sin.

Clothes are just not worth all the trouble they cause. Look at what happened this week for instance. We are getting ready to take a little vacation trip. My husband, Lout, is being industrious for once, and he and his brothers, Leech and Lurch, are checking out the car. They even change the oil.

I figure I better get busy and start throwing dirty clothes in the washer. My little daughter, Gladiola, is whining she can't find her crayons, so I give her a eyebrow pencil to draw with. After I put the stuff in the dryer, she says she is tired of drawing everything brown, so I give her a red marker. It isn't until after I take the clothes out I found out where her crayons are. In the pocket of her little white sunsuit is where they are. But now they have melted, and Lout's T-shirts are blue-violet, brick red, sea green, and some other real picturesque colors. Also the kids' drawers and socks and my sexy slip with the knee slit.

I start wondering if I can convince everybody they look better that way. I could say we are all cheerful and bright from the inside out. But I decide that won't work, so I decide to put them back in the washer and give it my best shot.

What I don't know is that instead of dumping the oil down the sewer, Lout had gone inside and got my cooking funnel and funneled it into a empty bleach

bottle. Then he daintily perches it on top the garbage can. My son, Gargoyle, after getting yelled at a few times, goes to haul out the garbage. He sees this full bleach bottle there. And like a little angel he takes it inside and puts it where the bleach bottles belong, next to the washer.

You see where this is leading? I fill up the washer and, without stopping to measure (my mama told me always to measure, but did I listen?), I dump a quart of motor oil on the clothes.

So much for cheerful and bright from the inside out. So much for underwear.

But it's not the end. It gets worse. I am washing late into the night, of course. Around 11 P.M., with Lout and the boys still out in front talking about cars, I am staggering to the washer with my last load. The washer is in the garage, which is attached to the house. Usually we don't even go out there at night. Because to turn on the light, you got to walk in the middle of the room and grope around for the light string, which you can never find unless it is daylight.

So I am out there in the pitch dark, and I put in the last load, and I remember I want to wash what I got on, so I just take it all off and throw it in. I know I left a bathrobe on top the clean clothes, but when I reach for it, I can't find it. Then my hand touches the light cord. I yank it.

Which is when I find out Lout left the garage door up. And there they are—Lout, Leech, Lurch— standing in the driveway with their eyes bugging out. I scream and clutch the wash basket in front of me and run out. Lout said later I looked just like a bubble dancer when I did that.

Maybe I just as soon join the nudists. It won't be nothing new.

# Lout's Fuzzy, Wuzzy Disaster

This all started because my mother-in-law, Miss Larda, is terrified of burglars.

My friend Awlette tells her that the first thing a burglar does after he breaks in is go to the kitchen and steal the butcher knives so they can stab you in your bed. But instead of just locking them up, like most people would do, Miss Larda gives hers away and gets a food processor to use instead. My husband Lout says it is not a bad idea because there is so much of Miss Larda it would take a burglar a year to process her to death.

And she hides her money under her mattress. But Awlette says burglars always look there. So now every night she leaves a five-dollar bill in the knife drawer and a note that says, "This is where I hide my money. Do not come in the bedroom as I got a fatal disease."

Then she starts worrying about me. My husband, Lout, likes to play poker and go bowling at night—which I don't complain about because it keeps him out from underfoot. But she has to start in on him about not being around to protect me and his little

family. So he decides to surprise me with a dog. He might as well have surprised me with a snake.

I look at it and do I see a cute puppy? No. I see a hairball that wets. But the kids never had a dog before and they are falling all over this one. Gladiola, the baby, she has even named him—"Fuffy." She is trying to say "Fluffy," I guess, but it comes out "Fuffy."

Anyhow, Fuffy grows from a little hairball into a

big hairball and then a gargantuan hairball. I think he looks like a grizzly bear that needs a haircut. But he has a problem. His voice don't change. He will thunder across the floor at somebody he don't trust—like the roach man, for instance—but, when he should go "wooof, grufff, woooof" and terrify the roach man, he goes "yip, yipe, squeak" in a falsetto and the roach man laughs.

Now, Lout don't have anything against roach men, but he don't like the idea of having one laugh at his dog. Lout thinks he has got a macho image to maintain. Once he got furious at me just because I hung little Gladiola's pink flowery diaper bag on the gun rack in the cab of this used pickup he drives around in. He don't even have a gun and this rack is a perfect place for a diaper bag because, when you hang it up, the bottle in it stays standing up and don't leak. But no, a gun rack has got to have a gun or nothing.

So he gets real upset about this poor dog with a high voice. He says there must be something wrong with Fuffy's glands and he decides to take him to the vet to get them adjusted. Fuffy don't like the idea. But Lout just pulls him in the truck cab by his leash and hooks the leash over the gun rack. It is summer and usually in summer Lout keeps his truck windows rolled up because he wants to look like he's got air conditioning. That's part of his image too, I guess. But Fuffy hasn't had a bath in a while, so Lout decides to roll down the window this time. That turns out to be a mistake. As soon as Lout stops at a light, Fuffy jumps out the window. Lout is busy watching two cops on the other side of him and hoping they don't notice his brake tag is expired. So he don't see Fuffy go. Anyway, Fuffy don't go far because the leash stops him short with only the tips of his hind feet touching the ground. When Lout starts up, Fuffy has no choice but to run alongside on his tiptoes. Thank God he thinks to bark. Lout looks over and sees this frantic hairy face staring in the window and he slams on the brakes. This causes two things. The leash breaks and the cops sit up and pay attention. Fuffy, who is no fool, runs under the nearest front porch. Lout pulls over and runs after him, bellowing, "Fuffy! Get back here!"

Lout is crouching next to the porch, yelling, "Fuffy! Fuffy! Fuffy!" and he hears this deep voice behind him say, "Did you wose your wittle doggie? And do you know your bwake tag has expired?"

Lout always says there is nothing he hates worse than cop sarcasm. He pays for a brake tag and a ticket with the money he was going to pay the vet. (He also gets a lecture on cruelty to animals because a old lady on that front porch tells the police Lout was dragging the dog along the street.) Anyway, Lout decides that if this dog can't bark right, he just as soon not bark at all. Now when the roach man comes around, Lout sticks a muzzle on Fuffy and tells him this is a vicious dog named Rambo. Fuffy don't answer to the name Rambo, but Lout says that is all right because he is never going to speak to him again anyway.

# Pantyhose and
# Basketball Bellies

~~~~~~~

**H**aving a baby is like getting a tattoo. It hurts so bad at the time, you decide you only want one.

Of course, before you have a baby, you usually got months of walking around looking like a weather balloon. Now, I know some really dainty types, who never look like they got anything worse than a little water retention and then one day they come trotting home with this brand-new baby. It's enough to make you believe in the stork.

Me, I look pregnant right from the start. I wake up the morning after and I look five months along. I don't even need to go ask the doctor. I got people making bets on whether it's going to be twins before I even buy my prenatal vitamins.

The first time I get pregnant, my mother-in-law, Miss Larda, brings over this bottle of lotion they call Mother's Friend. She says I should rub it thoroughly over my abdomen each morning to avoid unsightly stretch marks.

At that point, I don't know if I much care how sightly my stomach is when all this is over, but I do what she says. The next morning I slather it on. Then I try to put on my pantyhose. Now, getting pantyhose to stay put on a stomach shaped like a basketball is quite a trick under normal circumstances. But once you got the thing greased, you got no chance whatever. The pantyhose lose. Like Lout said, watching me, modern technology is defeated by a old-fashioned remedy. So I wind up safety-pinning them to my bra, which makes me walk sort of bent over, but everybody walks funny when they are pregnant.

As you get bigger and bigger, you notice people around you start acting funny—like you are a big egg getting ready to hatch any minute. You walk into a party and everybody feels inspired to say stuff like, "Uh-oh. I don't know anything about delivering babies. Are you sure you're okay?" (Like if you were in the last stages of labor, you'd be standing there eating potato chips and thinking about how surprised they were all going to be in a couple of minutes.) If a roach scurries over your foot you just got to be quiet about it, because if you let out a squeal everybody will come unglued and try to rush you to the hospital.

My mother and Miss Larda are full of childbirth

stories that I don't want to hear. They all got phrases like "suffered the tortures of hell" in them. That don't make me feel no better.

So I sign up for this course where they teach you

how to have a baby by breathing deep. A whole room-ful of women breathing deep together sounds like a convention of obscene phone callers, but just the same, I begin to see the point.

I also learn not to say "bad labor pains," but "good labor contractions," and to remain calm and in control at all times.

Anyway, I wake up at 2 A.M. one morning and the good contractions are coming every two minutes, so I calmly bend over Lout's ear and yell, "This is IT! NOW! Move IT!" That's a good way to remain in control of Lout. He shoots out of bed like a snake was in it. I control him all the way to the hospital by saying things like, "Faster! I'm going to have this kid right here! I shoulda gone in the convent!" and stuff.

But we get there in time for me to have our daughter Gumdrop. When they bring me to my hospital room after I have her, Miss Larda is already there waiting. She has brought a jar of her oyster soup, to build up my strength, and a magazine. On the back of the magazine is a ad that reads, "Have a Camel," and I say, "No way! A seven-pound baby is plenty." And then I think about how big baby elephants are and I figure I know why mother elephants just stay pregnant for two years. They are getting up their nerve.

But evidently I don't got a memory like a elephant because what do I do but have another baby pretty soon, and another one after that.

I better not start with no tattoos.

# Incident at the Black Velvet Shower

What are you supposed to do when somebody decides to show up at your house for a visit and don't tell you ahead of time? You don't even have a chance to hide the dirty dishes in the oven and kick a few things under the couch. I know some people get away with crouching under the windowsills and pretending they aren't home. That don't work for me because, as soon as somebody knocks, one of my kids throws open the door—all smiles—and says, "Come right on in. Mom's on the toilet." Or something like that. I have just learned to live with it. Surprise company deserve what they get.

Still, I feel bad about Sister Ignacita.

Of course, it wasn't my fault. The blame goes to

my two no-good brothers in-law and their black velvet shower. You want to know how this connects up with a nun? You'll never believe it.

Sister Ignacita is really my cousin Ignacita, who went to the convent right after high school. We look sort of alike, and she used to get in trouble a lot for things, like talking to her neighbor and being tardy, when it was really me that did it. I guess she figured if she started wearing a habit, nobody would mix us up anymore.

Anyway, I have no idea she is in town. I have other things to worry about. Leech and Lurch are living in the other half of the double we are living in. And when my son, Gargoyle, tells me he asked to use Uncle Lurch's bathroom and saw this shower done in black velvet, I am not hardly surprised. That's about their kind of taste. Now, I never said I was no interior decorator, but I got a painting of Elvis on velvet that is absolutely beautiful. I know good taste. And black velvet in the shower is not good taste. It is weird.

Come to find out, the shower isn't black velvet. It's just never been cleaned since them two slobs moved in. Of course, I don't find out until they decide to move out and they hire Lout to clean it all up so they can get their deposit back.

Lout starts spraying out the shower with some little pansy-smelling type of spray can. Then he decides to blast it out. He goes outside and gets the hose and feeds it through the window. Then he screws the power nozzle on it. Then he strips off his clothes and yells for me to go outside and turn on the water and bring him a towel.

I don't have no towels clean, so I bring him our barbecue tablecloth, which is made out of terrycloth. Then I go off to the grocery.

I don't know firsthand what happens after that, but this is what I figure. Lout must decide to take a break and puts down the hose. This hose, turned on full force with a power nozzle on it, takes on a life of its own. It dances around and sprays the bathroom and the bedroom, with Lout chasing it, and it finally lunges back out the window.

About this time, Sister Ignacita is coming up the walk. Lout grabs the tablecloth, which has "Come and get it!" printed across the middle. He wraps it around him and runs outside, past Sister Ignacita, who he mistakes for me.

He turns off the water, feeds the hose back in through the window, and runs back inside. He passes her again and yells, "Turn that water back on and then get in this bedroom. I need you!" The water comes back on, but nobody comes to mop up the bedroom.

When I get home, he asks where I've been. I've been making groceries, I tell him. So who turned on the water?

We find out later when we get a nice note from Sister Ignacita that says we strengthened her commitment to her vocation.

Lout is worried, but I tell him, "No, anything you do to keep a nun in the convent is got to be a good thing." And if the sight of him running around in a "Come and get it!" tablecloth was enough to do it, then he should think of himself as a instrument of the Lord. He thinks that is a compliment, poor heart.

# Gargoyle's Shoes for School

I ought to be down on my knees giving thanks.
School is getting ready to start. But I ain't too
grateful. I guess animal tamers get used to walking
into a cage full of lions and I get used to walking into
a house full of kids.

Besides, I remember myself those last days of
summer, counting the days you had left, praying like
anything that this year you weren't going to get the
meanest teacher in school. Ours was Sister Gargantua.
Seven feet tall. Never raised her voice—just growled,
deep in her throat, like a pit bull. Picture that scene
in *Star Wars* where the door swings open and Darth
Vader stalks in through swirls of smoke and towers

over the rebel fighters. That was Sister Gargantua coming into the fourth-grade classroom.

One Christmas, my friend Awlette gave Sister Gargantua a canister of homemade cookies. She ate it too, Awlette said. Can and all.

My kids don't have to worry about Sister Gargantua. She ain't around no more. Or maybe she is, hanging upside down in a cave somewheres.

But things are different now. Last year, my son Gargoyle's teacher, Miss Whimp, acts like she is the one who is terrified. Take, for instance, the time he packed his own lunch. That day, he asks if he can take some leftovers from supper. I am busy combing breakfast out of little Gladiola's hair, so I don't argue.

But a couple hours later, I get a call from Miss Whimp. Gargoyle and his science class have left for a morning field trip. His lunch box is on his desk and something red is oozing out it and drip, drip, dripping onto the floor. I think she got suspicions there is a amputated body part or something in there.

So I got to go to the school and open the lunch box, which turns out to be full of leftover spaghetti sauce. Gargoyle didn't bother with Tupperware, he just poured it straight on in, so when he set the lunch box on its side it started leaking. Now, Sister Gargantua would never have turned a hair, even if she had any. She'd probably have intoned the rite of burial and flung it out the window. But Miss Whimp is another story.

I don't know who he'll get this year, but I hope

it's somebody who knows how to handle herself in combat. Anyway, I got other problems. Like shoes for school.

One hot day in August, I call my kids in to go shopping. Gargoyle is muttering something about how medicine men in Africa walk on hot coals and don't need no shoes, but I don't pay no attention. That is a mistake.

At the store, the salesman takes off Gargoyle's shoe. Then he leaps back. From across the room, he says, "When's the last time you *changed* those socks, kid?" (I find out later, when I got a good grip on his neck, that Gargoyle has been working up to walking on hot coals barefoot by walking over cold soot from the barbecue pit in his sock feet.)

But I know the shoe salesman must think I never washed this kid's socks in my life. So I got to impress him with how good a mother I really am. I buy the best shoes they got. Scuffproof toes. Reinforced heels. They probably got diamond insets in the soles, from the price. And in October, they fall apart. School shoes are programmed to destruct in thirty days.

I admit it don't help that it is against my kids' principles to ever touch shoes with their hands. In the morning, they find a shoe wherever it landed when they kicked it off the day before. Then they nudge it along with their toe until they get it over against the wall. Then, they shove their whole foot into it and step down, so they cave in the back. Then they go off happy in a pair of forty-dollar shoes they have transformed into bedroom slippers.

I'll tell you this. It is against my principles to buy two pairs of shoes for the same kid in one year. So, I get out the black electric tape. I can get real creative with that stuff. I create black stripes along the ripped-out seams and, after a while, black soles. Before school is over the kids' feet look like they been mummified in black, but I don't spend another forty dollars on shoes.

And I bet Sister Gargantua would agree with that.

# How to Out-Tidy a Tideybole

There are two kinds of neighbors you can have. The kind with junk cars all over their lawn and window screens pushed out and stuff dangling from the rafters that you don't even want to ask what it is. These are the good kind.

And then there's the kind with a lawn that looks like it has been cut with a manicure scissors and the front door polished and the curtains at the windows white as the driven snow. They are the bad kind.

I got a set of each, one on each side of me. The first set I call the Scumms. They got three pet dogs, two pet cats, and a bunch of mice that ain't pets. They also got kids—about as many as they got mice. And they either got a pig or one of the kids is pretty funny-looking.

The ones on the other side are the Tideyboles: Lysolla and her husband Nerd and their ten-year-old daughter Pristine. You know the type—Lysolla starches her bras to make them iron better; Nerd goes to the park to wash his car so he don't get the driveway

damp; Pristine puts on a apron to eat a Popsicle—that kind of stuff.

The Scumms are good neighbors because no matter how terrible your house looks, theirs is worse. I get my Christmas decorations down by Mardi Gras at least, but they put Christmas lights up five years ago and they're still up. The grandmother plugs them in every night, thinking it is the TV. Then she complains the set is broken and goes to bed, so they don't tell her nothing. But they don't turn off the lights neither. You see them in August, twinkling around the masking tape on the windows that probably dates back twenty-one years to Hurricane Camille. Sometimes I can spend a whole day staring over at their house and mine seems cleaner by the minute without me ever picking up a thing.

But looking at the Tideyboles' house is as depressing as looking at a *Playboy* centerfold. Because I know that no matter how hard I work at it, what I got ain't never going to look that good.

I got kids who got the Midas touch in dirt. Anything they pick up, they stain. I got a husband who thinks the best way to eat dry cereal is to sprawl out in front of the TV, open the box, and chug-a-lug it like beer. I got a survival sofa. If we was stranded with nothing but the sofa, we could stay alive for a week just on what's in it. Anything you need to sustain a human life you can find somewhere under them cushions.

But even if I got my house cleaned up for the Pope, it still wouldn't look as good as the Tideyboles' looks when the Orkin man walks in.

For one thing, Pristine has learned how to sleep in a bed without messing it up. She showed Gargoyle how she does this. She just sort of squats on the pillow, oozes under the covers, don't move a muscle for eight hours, and then oozes out again in the morning. And the bed still looks made. After Gargoyle has slept in a bed, it looks like there was one of them mud-wrestling matches in it.

Maybe I could take all this better if Lysolla didn't always have to be telling me about all her little routines that keep her house so nice. On Wednesday, she shines the tub with Jubilee kitchen wax. On Thursday, she turns the mattresses and sprays them with mattress freshener. Friday is wax-the-garage-floor day.

Only one time—one time—did I ever get one up on her. I will always remember that day. It is Sunday, the toilet won't flush, and Gargoyle is missing his little robot-that-turns-into-a-baby-machine-gun, which he left on the back of the seat. We only got one toilet, so this is a emergency that is getting worse by the minute. We try with the plumber's friend and we try with a hanger, but we can't get it unstuck.

Finally Lout unbolts the whole thing and drags it outside and I get out the garden hose. So there I am in the front yard, holding a hose in the toilet, waiting for a robot or a machine gun to wash out. And along comes Lysolla, just getting home from church with Nerd and Pristine in tow. Of course, she asks what in the world I am doing.

I guess I got a mean streak I didn't know about, or I guess the devil makes me do it. What I do, I raise my eyebrows, and I say, "What do you mean, what am I doing? Don't *you* deep-clean your toilet every Sunday?"

And I watch her go in her house and I hear her yell for her husband. I know Nerd is going to be busy with the pipe wrench in a minute. And for once, looking at her house, I feel good.

# Italian Food and
# Vampire Dreams

~~~~~~~~

I t is a dark and stormy night. Maybe not stormy. But dark. Plenty dark. And I should have my head examined for sitting up and watching that vampire movie after everybody else is asleep. Let me tell you right now I am not superstitious. But tonight, I start thinking, it wouldn't hurt to keep a little cross by my bed in case I want to pray all of a sudden. And a little garlic, to keep from catching a cold. So I root around and I find Gumdrop's little rosary, which has a cross. I am out of garlic, but I got a shaker of garlic powder, so I take that. And I lock the doors and the windows. I check all my kids plus our little next-door neighbor, Pristine, who is spending the night with my daughter Gumdrop.

Pristine is a only child and her mama, my neighbor Lysolla, never let her sleep away from home before. But finally her mama said she could stay with us because Gumdrop's room is just across the alley from Lysolla's own bedroom. And Lysolla can look out the window and blow a goodnight kiss to little Prissy. My son Gargoyle says that is disgusting and girls are nothing but nosy pests. And he has locked himself in his room.

He is still there. The other kids are asleep looking innocent, even the baby, Gladiola, with her little tush stuck up in the air. My husband, Lout, is lying in bed like a dead man. I give him a kick and he snorts so I know he is alive. So finally I pull on my nightgown and crawl in next to him. Nervous as I am, I doze off and I don't hear Gargoyle go down the hall to the bathroom.

But about that time, my brother-in-law, Lurch, who is feeling no pain, like usual, is discovering his mama has locked him out. So he shuffles down the block to our house to sleep on our couch. Whatever he has drunk that evening has slowed his reflexes down. So when he knocks, he don't knock-knock-knock like people usually do, but he does it loud and slow. *Knock*, and then a pause, and then *knock*, and then a pause, and then *knock*. I sit up straight in bed and I feel my hairs turning white one a time. I kick Lout, but he just snorts again. And I realize I am going to have to handle this myself.

I grab the rosary and go to sling it around my neck, so I'll have both hands free, but it is a little

kid's rosary and it just rests on my head like a hat,
with the cross hanging on the side of my face. I don't
stop to worry about that. I take the garlic powder and,
as I creep down the hall, I pick up the Holy Bible off
the bookstand. I am ready now. Very slowly, I open
the door a crack. And there ain't nobody there.

This is because Lurch has got tired hanging

around and decided to go around the side of the house
and climb in a window. His mistake is to pick Gumdrop's window. Across the alley, Lysolla is on the alert.

As soon as Lurch drags up a garbage can to stand
on to get up to the window, Lysolla leaps into action.
She throws up her own window and yells, "Fire!"
(Because she heard somewhere that if you yell "Bur-
glar!" nobody will come, but they will come for a fire.)
She also grabs the can of Mace she keeps on her bed

table and let loose with it. It don't do too much good because you are supposed to spray it in the person's eyes and she is spraying Lurch's back. But the commotion wakes up little Gladiola, who starts up a wail that sounds like an ambulance coming.

I recognize that screech and rush back down the hall. I see the light under the bathroom door and I think the vampire or somebody must have Gladiola in there. The door is locked, so I thunk on it with the Bible. Gargoyle assumes Pristine is doing this and he yells, "Go away! This is *my* bathroom!" But I can't hear him because I am screaming, "Leave my baby go!"

I don't know how long all this went on "Fire!" "This is *my* bathroom!" and "Leave my baby go!" but, eventually, Lurch gets tired fooling with the window, so he just steps down and curls up on the ground to go to sleep. Lysolla calls 911 and says she has killed a man.

But when the cops get there, the body is gone. Lurch has roused himself and gone home. Pristine has been taken away by Lysolla and I have beat open the bathroom door and found Gargoyle, who thinks I have turned into a religious fanatic. And there is garlic powder spilled all over the house. I try to explain and I don't know if the police believe me or not.

The next morning Lout wakes up, takes a deep breath, and tells me he's hungry. He dreamed about Italian food all night, he says. I tell him that the next vampire who comes by can have him.

# Modine's Attic
# Christmas Adventure

~~~~~~~

The only thing worse than a reformed cigarette smoker is a early Christmas shopper. Like my mother-in-law, Miss Larda. She prances into my house the day after Thanksgiving and looks at me lying on my couch trying to recover from twenty-four hours of straight cooking followed by twenty-four more hours of stuffing my face. And she says, "Well, Modine, you finished your Christmas shopping?" Which, of course, I ain't even started to think about and don't want to think about.

She finished hers in August. The Queen of Smug, that's her. Of course, back in July when it is so hot we are all either under water or leaning up against a air conditioner, she goes around like a busy little elf

~~~~~ 75 ~~~~~

and writes down everybody's Christmas wish. But in December, when we all open our presents and find stuff like frog flippers, inflatable alligator floats, and flip-flop sandals, we ain't too thrilled. Except for Lout. He is as happy with his six-pack as he would have been back in July when he asked for it.

I can't shop early anyways because my kids can't

decide between TV commercials. In September, little Gladiola wants Dolly Surprise. (The surprise is that her hair grows. She don't, thank God, give you the kind of surprises real babies do.) In October, she switches to Barbie Babysits, a set with a Barbie doll and a little plastic baby. (Lout calls this "Barbie Gets Knocked Up," but I tell him not to talk like that.) In November, she decides on a Teenage Mutant Ninja Turtle. But come December, she tells me, with a big trusting smile, that Santa Claus is going to bring her a Talking Alf doll. And she tells me this at the exact minute and hour and second that every Talking Alf in the country is sold out—except one. That one goes on sale at the Maison Blanche across the river at eight in the morning two days before Christmas and thirty other people are rushing over there to buy it. I am the one to get it. I ain't going to tell you how. I'll just say that sometimes you got to be vicious, especially if it's Christmas.

So, finally, it is Christmas Eve. My kids are lying all snug in their beds, with visions of presents dancing in their heads, while my husband Lout in his underwear has curled up to sleep like a old grizzly bear.

I am up in the attic, getting all the presents ready to haul down. I got to explain this. We got a little spring ladder that leads to the attic. You pull it down by a cord when you want to go up there and, when you finish and come down, you just give it a shove and it snaps up. I don't know to this day who gave it that shove, or if it was just the house settling, or what, because it never happened before or since. But all of a sudden it slams shut and I am up in the attic, in the dark, with the Christmas presents. Lucky I am not one that is afraid of closets—you know, like those people that got closetraphobia—so I don't panic. I ain't afraid of attics either. But that don't mean I want to celebrate my Christmas Eve up there.

I start thinking. If I push down hard on the trapdoor, I will get down all right, but I will probably break my neck. If I yell and scream the kids will wake and they'll find out the truth about Santa Claus. I finally decide to start crawling toward the sound of Lout's snoring. When I figure I am about over him, I take off my shoe and I pound with the heel. The snoring stops and I hear this strangling sound, so I guess I must've knocked some plaster down. He gets quiet and I can picture him looking up with this puzzled expression he has, like a dog when it gets gum in its mouth. And then he says, in this groggy voice, "Santa?"

This gets me mad and I say, "No, you idiot. Modine! Get me out!" But I am whispering, so I don't wake up the kids, and he can't hear me. Then he wakes up a little more and what does he do but get it in his head that I am a burglar. I hear a scramble and he yells, "I got a gun here! Come out with your hands up!" Like a burglar is going to break in the house, pull down the attic stairs, climb up there, crawl over our bed, and pound. I yell *"This is Modine!"* and a few other things that, being a lady, I won't repeat. Finally he opens the attic and, of course, the kids are all awake now. But I think fast and invent a story about how Santa mistook the air vent in our attic for a chimney, put the presents through there, and how I had to go get them. They believe it. They'll believe anything as long as they get their loot. You know, I think Lout believes it too.

# There's Worse Things than Wet Feet

My mother-in-law don't believe germs cause disease. She believes it is drafts. Or a "chill." I have had to leap out of bed at 5:30 in the morning on the coldest day of the year to catch the phone and hear her telling me it's cold out and I should be sure the kids have a hot breakfast and wear their thermal underwear so they won't catch their deaths. I told her I never knew death was contagious. But instead of taking it as sarcastic, like I mean it, Miss Larda just starts naming all the people she knows that passed on before their time because they went out on a cold day without their knit caps. She has cousins dead from that. Or if it wasn't that they died of, it was from catching a cold in the bowels. You get that from going out in cold weather without your thermal underwear and then sitting down, like on the curb or something. I never asked what are the symptoms of a cold in the bowels because I don't want to know.

She also believes rain kills. If it's raining, you got to drive the kids to school and, instead of dropping them off in front, you got to park somewheres and walk them in so you can hold a umbrella over their heads. I say I am probably going to catch my death from getting hit by a truck crossing the street bent over trying to hold a umbrella over three kids at once. She says if I'm going to die, I might as well die with my kids dry.

The other things that can kill you are biting your fingernails (blood poisoning), going out in the night air (I guess you evaporate or something), and, worst of all, constipation. She's got lots of cousins who died of that, she says. So what she does, she brings me over a ten-pound bag of dried prunes she got at Schwegmann's and tells me to make sure the kids eat some every morning with breakfast. Just to keep the peace, I try it. I get away with it for a while by telling the kids they are Texas raisins, but they catch on to that and tell me they will never, never trust me again and I have to throw the rest out.

Miss Larda is always warning me not to do things that cause sterility—like carrying heavy things and pushing furniture around the room and turning mattresses by yourself. I tried them all, but none of them worked. Which goes to show she don't know as much as she thinks. But my husband Lout believes all this like it is a religion. Lout has never seen the light of day without his undershirt on. Lout likes to go around acting like he's macho, but deep down underneath all that hair and lard, he secretly thinks he is in delicate health.

I get the flu, I live with it. I cook with it, I clean with it, I go to work with it, I *share* it. Lout gets the

flu, he acts like it is his last day on earth. "I got my affairs in order, Modine," he tells me in a gravelly voice, while he's climbing into the bed. "You and the kids won't have nothing to worry about." (What this means is that the rent is paid and there's gas in the car. He don't have any affairs that I know about. I did see him making goo-goo eyes at the lady over at the drugstore up the street, but I thought, at the time, he was just trying to get a cheaper price on his beer.)

Anyways, Miss Larda rushes over with a jar of her oyster stew. (Some people get better on chicken soup, but with Lout it's oyster stew. Although he always likes to eat a couple of fried chickens to build up his strength.) And she blames me for him getting sick in the first place. "Did you make him wear his undershirt, Modine?" she asks me. "What does he wear on his feet when it's raining?"

She makes me feel so guilty I actually decide to buy him a pair of them waterproof rubber things that slip over your shoes. I remember the drugstore had them on sale a while back, but I don't know if they have any to fit his big size 13½ feet.

I go over there and I don't see them so I walk to the back to ask the lady if they got any left—even though I feel like a fool buying these for a grown man. So I say, sort of low, "You still got rubbers?" And she whispers. "Sure, sweetheart. What brand you like?" And I says, "I don't care what brand, but I need them big. Size extra large if you got it." "Well, honey, they only come in one size," she says to me, "but we never had no complaints." And then she reaches underneath the counter and what she pulls out I am embarrassed to tell you, but they were not for Lout's *feet*. I tell her to forget it. And I'll tell you this. If I ever catch him making goo-goo eyes at her again, what I'll give him will be worse than a cold in the bowels.

# Modine's Lifetime Supply of Drawers

I can't believe what I read in the papers. Reviews of Carnival parades. Like they was movies or something. Saying how colorful this or that one was and how good the bands played or didn't play and how artsy the whole thing was. Like anybody cares. There's only one way to judge a parade—by how much they throw. I don't care if them riders are hanging on to garbage trucks. If they are out there throwing, I am out there with my Schwegmann's bag catching.

If I want color I can turn on the TV. If I want music I got the stereo. If I want art I can go look at them framed pictures they got at the K & B. But what I want from parades is cups and beads and doubloons and whatever else they got that is free.

One thing I got in common with my husband's family, the Gunches. When it comes to getting stuff at parades, we got true talent. On a good night, we can hit three parades and fill up a entire back seat with stuff. Sometimes we put a cigar box up on a stick, sometimes we hold up signs that say, "Hi! I Am a Rich Tourist From Alaska." Sometimes we just wave the baby around.

But I'll tell you one thing. We got standards. We do not bring along crutches or sit there in a wheelchair unless one of us actually did sprain a ankle or something. Maybe I might limp a little when I'm chasing a float, but that's about as far as I go. You got to draw the line.

One thing that never happened before is that somebody in the family actually got to ride in a parade. Not until last year, when my husband Lout's bachelor friend named Railbird tells Lout about a guy he knows who rides every year. But this year the guy comes into some money and he decides to get snotty and go skiing up at Aspen instead. That is something I will never understand. Freezing your tush off on a mountain somewheres when you could freeze it right here at home and at least have some beads to show for it. So let him break his legs. It means Lout gets to take his place on the float, next to Railbird.

Railbird is going on about how great it is to throw stuff instead of catch it. He even quotes from the Bible about casting your bread on the waters and getting it back a hundredfold. This don't sound like Railbird, but I don't worry about it.

Lout is so excited it don't even bother him that the theme of this parade is Kiddies' Caboodle and he and Railbird have to dress up like Little Bo Peep, with calico dresses and bloomers and long blonde curls. He even asks his mama, Miss Larda, to make him and Railbird little calico purses that they can wear dangling from their wrists on a ribbon.

Me and Miss Larda and all the Gunches—Leech and Lurch and Larva and the kids, of course—decide to make sure Lout don't miss us in the crowd. We all are going to dress in Mardi Gras colors. We get bright yellow ponchos and purple baseball caps. And we build a ladder seat for the kids and we tell Lout what corner we going to be at. We get to this parade early, all set to be drowned in Mardi Gras throws.

Lout is ready too. Too ready. Just before our

corner he sees this bunch of people dressed in purple and gold. But what he don't see, because he and Railbird have been sipping at these pints of gin in their little calico purses, is that this group of people is not us. It is a bunch of LSU fanatics. They dress in purple and gold all year long, I guess. And Lout throws them the artificial rose that was suppose to be for me and his plastic cups and the long beads he got for his mama and the little stuffed teddy bear in a cellophane bag that was for our little Gladiola and everything else that was for us. *Then* he sees us.

Well. I know that I got grounds for divorce. But Lout, for once, is thinking fast. He grabs Railbird's sack of throws—I don't think Railbird even notices this, he got his calico purse upside down over his head—and Lout dumps everything on us. But what Railbird has in there—which comes floating down—is twenty dozen bikini panties with Railbird's phone number on them in big red print. This is what he meant by getting it back a hundredfold.

Then a miracle happens. The next float is loaded with more LSU fanatics. They see us in our purple and gold and they go crazy. We wind up with five little stuffed tigers, twelve gross of purple and gold long beads, six pennants, and seventeen key chains.

Anyway, I decide to stay married. At least I am not going to run out of drawers any time soon. Let Railbird wonder why his social life dried up.

# How to Catch
# a Man

I am watching *Facts of Life* the other day and I am wondering what kept me out of trouble when I was fifteen. And I know what it was. Two things. Braces on my teeth and mortal sin. Even if some boy had got past the way I looked (like a Edsel with zits) and let his animal nature get aroused, like Sister Gargantua said, I was supposed to realize he was a Occasion of Sin and belt him one.

It was not such a bad system. Now they got invisible braces. And they don't believe in mortal sin no more. My mother-in-law says all you can do is fall down on your knees and pray to God your daughter has bad breath.

My little girl Gumdrop is a cheerleader for Celibacy Academy. Them cheerleaders don't wear no baggy sweaters and long skirts like they used to back when I was in Catholic girls' school. Nuh-uh. They wear these little skirts as short as a tutu and a little top like a vest with no shirt. And they don't just jump up and down and go rah-rah. They do these

things called hip rolls, which is a movement I didn't even know existed until after I was married.

But I'll tell you, when I was fifteen, we didn't worry none about getting P.G., or catching one of them transmission diseases you get from sex. We knew we wouldn't live long enough. If we committed a mortal sin, like kissing a boy for longer than thirty seconds or wearing immodest shoes that showed the cleavage of our toes, a bus would hit us on our way to church to go to confession and that would be it. If God was in a bad mood, we could get struck down for even *thinking* about doing something like that. Sister Gargantua warned us we'd go straight into the flames of hell for all eternity—on a technicality.

And if you wasn't allowed to think about s-e-x, then you couldn't ask any questions. I got my sex education from the underwear and hernia section of the Sears catalog.

But some things don't change. Every few months, the nuns give a little speech about inviting a nice young man to the school dance. Which was asking the impossible. At a all-girls school, you don't get too much chance to meet any kind of young man. After a while, the guy who sweeps up the place after hours starts to look good. At least he got hair on his legs.

Meanwhile, over at the boys' school, which I will call Holy Repression Prep, home of about five hundred hairy-legged Occasions of Sin, the same thing was going on in reverse. My husband, Lout, remembers them days. He says after a while he was eyeing up his friends' mothers when they come in for teachers' conferences. He said this one guy named Larry had a ol' lady with knockers that was the talk of the school.

At the girls' school, when it gets close to the time of the dance, you figure you got a choice. Get hold of a boys' high school yearbook and start calling everybody in it, beginning with the letter A. Or get fixed up with a blind date. The person who does the fixing up always says the same thing. "Don't bother looking him up in the yearbook—the picture's no good. Besides, he's got a wonderful personality."

I remember my senior year. I am so desperate for a date to the Senior Prom, I decide to make a sacrificial offering. (Catholics do this sometimes. Other people mostly try a lucky rabbit's foot or just plain pray.) I walk around with a rock in my shoe for a entire week. And it works. Hanna Bunkart, a girl who could find a eligible man if she was stranded at a eunuchs' convention, fixes me up with a date. She says he looks like he'd be great at basketball. I think tall, so I buy real high heels—modest ones, of course, that don't show no cleavage. Our dance dresses have to pass inspection too. No strapless, no spaghetti straps. If the nice young man goes totally out of control, the nuns want us dressed in something that will hold up under assault.

On prom night, I answer the door and he is standing there, staring at the floor, with a corsage all rumpled up in his hand, and he says, "How-do-you-do-my-name-is-Lout-Gunch." And then he looks at me, in my modest shoes and attack-proof dress and, even dressed like that, I must look better than Larry's old lady because he smiles all over his face.

Me, I'm thinking Hanna must of meant he *looked* like a basketball. But still, he don't look so bad to me. And the rest is history.

But sometimes I wonder what would have happened if I kept that rock in my shoe for another week.

# Modine Makes
# Cow Pie
# Supreme

~~~~~

**Y**ou are always seeing cookbooks with cutesy names like *Joy of Pork Chops* or *101 Ways to Have Fun with Meat Loaf*. Why don't they tell it like it is? If they put out a book named *How to Make a Decent Dinner in Five Minutes Out of Whatever Is Lying Around*, it would be a bestseller. It would make whoever wrote it rich.

Maybe I will.

How can it miss? You know it yourself. You look through these cookbooks and you see these pictures of food where the peas look like they've been polished and they match the green checks in the tablecloth and the gravy on the rice goes with the napkin rings. And you think "Why don't I get off my lazy behind and make something looks that good?"

But there are two reasons why you don't. The first one is, at quarter after five on Wednesday when you just got home from work and there is nothing in the refrigerator but half a onion in a plastic bag, four slices of cheese somebody didn't wrap up right, and

a half bowl of cold spaghetti, the last thing you are thinking about is color coordinating the food.

The other thing is, if you got a husband like mine, you know he ain't really going to *taste* whatever you stick in front his face. My husband, Lout, he makes me think of a Great Dane to watch him eat. Once he starts, he don't stop. He might look up with this confused expression now and then, when he hits a chunk of something unusual, but he never stops chewing. In two minutes flat, he is done. He grabs his toothpicks and goes to watch the sports. So much for supper.

Now I admit, back when I first got married, I was a little worried about cooking. My mother-in-law is the kind who would fix three hot meals a day, all of them from scratch, all of them timed and seasoned perfect. I figured this man was brought up to be a gourmet. Actually, he was brought up to *think* he was a gourmet. I found that out after we was married a week. I had scorched something in a pot and I was boiling water and soap in it to loosen up the burnt stuff that was stuck to the bottom. Along comes Lout. He picks up a spoon. He opens up the lid. He tastes. And he don't retch. He don't gag. He don't even say, "Needs salt." He just looks over at me and he says, "When's supper?"

Then I know the truth. I can feed him anything.

Anybody else that married one like him can do it too.

So, all you got to do is grate up that onion and cheese, run next door and borrow a can of cream of mushroom soup, heat it all up together and pour it over your cold spaghetti, which by now you have turned into warmed-over spaghetti. You can call this little creation Wednesday Surprise. Or you can call it Tropicana Beach. Or you can shake some chili powder on it and call it Acapulco HaHa.

You got to be careful with the names though. One time, I had this fight with Lout and I felt sorry afterwards. So, I decide to make up and fix this special pie for dessert. It was from a recipe called "Moo-moo

Mousse" and the topping was ground up Milky Way candy bars. But I want him to think I made it up myself. So when he calls up and says, "What's for supper?" I make up a new name. "Cow Pie Supreme." I ain't from the country, so I didn't think nothing of it. But Lout, he spent some time on a farm with his cousins and they got a entirely different meaning for cow pies. So he figures I am *really* mad this time. So he never comes home. I have to go get him from his mama's the next day.

So you got to be careful of that. The other thing you got to do is keep up appearances. Even though your husband knows good and well that you got home from work fifteen minutes before he did, he wants to think you spent all day sweating in the kitchen for him.

So why fight it? Make everything *look* homemade. Open up two cans of Creole red beans and dump them in a big black pot. Now, throw a couple shakes of thyme in. (If you ain't got thyme, anything that looks like grass clippings will do.) And serve it on your instant rice.

For spaghetti, you open the jar and pour the sauce in the black pot. Get rid of the jar. Then you put some mushrooms in the microwave until they shrivel up a little and dump them in the sauce.

I can go on. Will this be a bestseller? I even got a idea for my next one. *The Joy of Making a Complete Meal During* Wheel of Fortune *Commercials*.

# Have Maytag, Will Travel

O n a gorgeous Saturday morning, when the sun is shining and the birds are singing and you can smell the flowers, my husband, Lout, always does the same thing. He walks outside and opens up the car hood and leans over and inhales fumes. He clanks around in there for a while, giving us all a view of his buns, and then he goes around and lays down next to the back of the car and oozes under it on his back until just his legs are sticking out. And if you go bend over and ask what is he doing he yells, "Gimme one of them wrenches from the garage. And pass by the kitchen and get me a beer."

After a while he comes inside and gets in the

shower and then he lays on the couch. That's his Saturday.

You would think from this that he is taking real good care of this car, so that the slightest little thing that could go wrong with it ain't going to go wrong. His mama thinks that. But I know better. I got to drive that car.

Not that I know much about cars. But I know this. I know that if it is raining and I am in the car and I am getting wet, then this car is leaking. The other day, it is pouring down rain when I come over the bridge and my whole left arm is sopping wet. I get home and I go give Lout a kick where he is lying on the couch and I say, "Look at here. My whole arm is wet." He sits up and he feels my arm and he says, "Did you roll up the window?" Like I am going to drive along in this monsoon, whining about how wet I am getting, but I am not going to roll up the window. Maybe I never got awarded no presidential scholarships or nothing, but what kind of I.Q. does this man think I have? So I say, "Lout, I thought of that. I rolled up the window." And he says to me, perfectly serious, "Are you sure you rolled it up all the way, Modine? Maybe you only rolled it up halfway."

I ain't going to tell you what happened after that.

One time we was having what Lout considers a serious problem with his van. It makes this little clicky sound about once every three blocks. This is a lot worse than a wife with a wet arm, according to Lout. To fix this you got to get up early and make a lot of racket outside so the neighbors will get mad. And if you told your wife you was going to spread fertilizer in the front yard, forget that. Leave that bag of fertilizer lie by the back door. You got important stuff to do.

So he is doing important stuff and I am sitting on the back steps and thinking about spreading that fertilizer on him, when he comes galloping through the gate. Lout don't never run so this is a surprise. He snatches up the fertilizer bag, throws it on his shoulder, and runs back out the gate with it. I am thinking, "Now what? He read my mind?" So I chase after him and when I come around the corner of the house, he is dumping the entire bag into the van motor. Come to find out, something in there caught on fire and he knew not to put water on a oil fire and the only thing he could think to smother it with was the fertilizer. Which is cow manure.

After that, we drive around smelling like a outhouse for Audubon Zoo. It ain't so bad when we first start the motor in the mornings. But as it heats up, the smell gets stronger. When we pull up to a traffic light people standing at the bus stop start checking the bottoms of their shoes. People in cars roll up their windows. That don't do no good because the smell comes in through the vents. Then they start sniffing their kids. Usually the light changes by that time, so we never get to see the end of all them little dramas we start.

Lout likes motors, but he is not one for cleaning the inside of a van. He says this is the beauty of van ownership. He can fill it up for years before he runs out of room. Beer cans. Old magazines. Carnival beads. He put our old washing machine in there to take to the dump, but then he found out the dump charges for dumping. So that Maytag stayed with us. Wherever we went, it went. It went to Disney World; it went to Dollywood; it went to The City of Snakes and Reptiles.

Then the van gets stolen. From right in front the house. Lout yells for me to call the police. I grab the phone and then I stop and think. I'm going to report a stolen vehicle with a washing machine and a beer can collection and a smell like a sewer. Finally, I just tell the police it is "loaded with all the extras." And we settle with the insurance people. But at night, I can look up and I know somewhere under that same sky, my Maytag is probably still seeing the world.

# Command
# Clothing

~~~~~~~~~~~~

At my house, clothes are communist. My T-shirt, for instance, don't belong to just me. It belongs to whoever gets out the house in it first. That goes for everything else—and most of my wardrobe got a better social life than I do. My Levis have sat on the front porch at Graceland. My bikini drawers ran up the aisle at that Duran Duran concert. And my blue sweatshirt been to Six Flags twice.

Where am I all this time? Home, looking for something to wear. And this is going to keep up just as long as baggy clothes stay in style. Because clothes can travel down, from big people to small people—but not up, from small people to me. My daughter Gumdrop thinks she looks just fine in my red turtleneck even though the armholes hit her at the elbows. But if I pull on her little red skirt, I look like I got on jogging shorts with no crotch.

Thank God for my husband Lout and his half of the closet. Last week, I realize all my clean shirts are out having a good time and I got nothing to wear to my cousin Loretta's wedding shower. I just grab his

big red sweatshirt. But I forget, until I am actually walking in the door, that it has "Trust me. I'm a gynecologist" printed on the front. Whoever said "Neither a borrower nor a lender be" probably had that happen to them.

Lout says his family had the same problem, only worse, when he was coming up. Instead of two kids and a baby, like we have, there was five kids and most of them eventually got to be the same size—extra large—and the same shape—round. There's Lout, of course, and his brothers, Leech and Lurch, and their sisters, Larva and Gloriosa. Gloriosa is the youngest and she turned out to be the family beauty. Oh, she has some fat on her all right, but it is all in the right places, if you know what I mean.

Anyway, the clothes-going-down rule worked out fine for Gloriosa. She could stick a belt or a sash on just about anything Larva owned and look great, but Larva couldn't fit in none of Gloriosa's stuff. This drove Larva right up the wall. So she did all kinds of things to keep Gloriosa out her clothes. She put her dresses in a garment bag and padlocked the zipper. She wrote "Larva's. Do not touch!" across all her underwear. She even labeled the soles of her socks and pantyhose.

Lout remembers the Friday evening Gloriosa was sitting, all dressed up, in the front room waiting for one of her boyfriends to pick her up. In comes Larva from her job at Burger King. Nobody knows to this day how Larva realized immediately that Gloriosa was wearing *her* pantyhose, but she let out a squeal like a car alarm and grabbed Gloriosa by the ankles and turned her upside down to read her name on the feet. Just then Gloriosa's date walked in. God only knows what he thought.

Most of the time though, Lout says, they was sneaky enough not to get caught. My kids are like that too. Gargoyle will be coming up the walk wearing my big beige pullover, which he has dribbled ketchup down the front of. But when he slips through the door, he is naked from the waist up and he has a beige lump stuck in his armpit. Sometimes this don't work though. Like the time Gumdrop went off in her brother's boxer shorts. She can't pull off the shorts in front the house, so she slips around back, climbs into Gargoyle's bedroom window, sticks the shorts in his drawer. What she forgets, though, is that she has sewed the front flap shut for the sake of modesty. And she has also put some little iron-on daisies over the stitching to make it cute. Naturally, Gargoyle don't examine his shorts the next day when he puts them on. So he don't discover this until he is in the boys' bathroom at school. A lot of his friends also discover it then, from what I understand.

Of course, all he can think of is revenge. He comes home with a black indelible marker and writes "FAT BUTT" across the back of her white shorts. But he makes a fatal error. Them shorts happen to be borrowed from me. So what they do, them two, is redecorate my shorts and wrap them up and give them to me for Mother's Day. Now when I wear them you can read "Number One Mom Number One Mom" on two hot-pink iron-on hearts real close together on my buns. But when I turn them inside out to wash, I can still see "FAT BUTT."

Now I know why communism don't work.

# I Never Sat
# on a Cat

Let me tell you right now that I am not no animal hater. Dogs, cats, pigs, little kids—it is all the same to me, as long as they know where to go to the bathroom. Unless they are roaches.

My daughter Gumdrop says if this is true, why can't she get a sweet little kitty? I say, get a goldfish. She says she can't *pet* a goldfish. I tell her, get a rubber glove.

If you really want to know, a sweet little kitty is just as much trouble as a teenage boy. And I already got one of them. But Gumdrop don't care about that. She just makes a sad face and I hear her telling her friends how her mama, for some reason, hates cats. I ask her, do I clutch myself and scream "Oh my God!" when a cat scurries across my steps? Do I run after it and stomp on it? Do I spray it with Pest Death? No. I do that for roaches. Not cats. And not teenage boys either. I don't hate them. I just don't want to support them both.

I'll tell you why. If you are giving free room and board to somebody, the least you could expect is a little groveling at your feet and a welcome-home slob-bering after a long day at work. But no, you come up the walk with plastic grocery bags hanging down from each elbow, kick at the door a while, and then dig out a key from the purse in your armpit, and stagger in. And there they are. The cat is lounging in the window staring at nothing and the teenager is lounging in front the TV staring at nothing. And they both slowly turn their heads, and they give you The Look. Like you are interrupting something crucial.

You walk into your own bathroom and there is the teenager counting his zits, and he says "Excuse me?" You stomp off to your bedroom and yank open your dresser drawer, and there is a cat reclining on your underwear, counting his whiskers. And he stares up at you with this same "Excuse me?" expression on his face.

You call either one by name and he don't hear. To get a sign of life, you got to rattle either a feeding dish or car keys.

Still, you are supposed to feed the cat, give him a nice, clean bed, haul him in for shots, and swear by his virtuous character when the neighbor lady complains he has got dishonorable intentions toward the little pussycat that lives at her house.

You catch my drift? But of course, before long I got a cat. It happens on a cold and stormy night, hard freeze expected. Everybody is supposedly in bed, and I am sitting peaceful and cozy in my furry slippers and

I am about to flick on the TV, when I hear this pathetic little "Mew? Mew?" at the door. And like a fool I get up and open the door and here is this little bitty brown-striped kitten, shivering, looking up at me with big round eyes. The rest is history. (Much later I find out the truth. Gumdrop got him that afternoon from her friend whose cat had kittens, and hid him in her bedroom until it was good and cold. Then she snuck out and left him on the doorstep, and she crouched in the bushes and mewed a few times. And I fell for it.)

But I'll tell you this, if he was a roach, I would never have took him in, freeze or no freeze. Which proves my point, not that anybody is listening.

So we name him Minny which is what you always call cats in New Orleans. We didn't know he was a boy at the time, but it don't matter, because who is going to tell *him* that Minny is not a boy's name?

Well, Minny is like a teenage boy, all right. He's even got a big fantasy life. Only instead of imagining whatever filth teenage boys think about, he makes believe he is a lion in the jungle. And I am a fat little antelope. So here I am, hauling a load of dirty clothes to the garage, and this ten-pound lion arches out from behind a couch cushion, lands on my leg, and swings around it like it was a maypole, and while I am going "Yaah!" and waltzing around with the laundry basket, he disappears underneath the TV.

I stagger to the kitchen to pour a cup of something to calm my nerves, and this lion goes back to being a snotty little cat. He comes strolling along with his tail held up straight, and sits down to lick his paws. And he turns his head and gives me The Look.

And I am thinking I should not have had that cat neutered. I should have had him drowned.

One thing that is not his fault is that his brown stripes are a exact match for our couch, which is his favorite reclining spot—when he can get to it before my son Gargoyle does. (Teenagers and cats recline. The rest of us just sit down.) Anyways, we have to look sharp whenever we sit there.

Of course, we all knew what was going to happen sooner or later. And it couldn't of happened to a better person—my neighbor Lysolla Tideybole, who had this habit of dropping over uninvited, so she could look down her nose at my housekeeping and give me smug advice. Anyhow, she prances in one fine Saturday afternoon to tell me what she uses to polish her doorknobs with, and she plops herself down on the couch and cat. Minny lets out a screech which probably sent dogs running under back steps for blocks around. Lysolla rises up and joins in with some of her own screeches. This don't help, because Minny has decided he is a lion, and he is going to hang on to her rear end until she drops from exhaustion, and then he is going to eat her. He don't let go until I dump a couple glasses of water on him, and then he skits under the couch and glares out, thinking, I guess, that one day he is going to have me taken out and boiled.

Lysolla puts her hand on my shoulder and stares into my eyes and she says, real sincere, "I *never* sat on a cat before." Like I am going to think maybe it's a habit. Then she don't say anything for a while, like she is reviewing her life, maybe, to be sure she didn't sit on just one cat. The answer is no, because she says it again. "*Never*. I *never* sat on a cat." She says it a few more times before she leaves, rubbing her backside.

My youngest daughter Gladiola uses "Never sat

on a cat" to show her nursery-school teacher she can rhyme. And Lysolla don't come back with her goody-two-shoes housekeeping talk for a long time. So I guess cats are worth something after all. It probably wouldn't have worked if she sat on my son.

# Never Answer the
# Phone Naked

It always happens when you are stark naked. You got everybody out the house, you got one foot in the tub, and the phone starts ringing. Now, you can be like my husband Lout, who just don't answer it because he figures it is going to be bad news or his mother; or you can be like me, who knows that the one time you don't answer the phone it will be the BIG ONE, the call from on high you been waiting for all your life—the one from Ed McMahon. Of course, it never is. For me, it's always Bob the Computer wants to sell me some aluminum siding. Or it's Lout's mother telling me her cousin Loona in Laplace finally had that baby and it's a thirteen-pound girl and wouldn't you know, that husband Loona married, he looks at the baby and says, "Give her a beard and we got Paul Prudhomme here," and Loona don't appreciate that . . . I am standing there turning blue wondering if I locked the front door and if that pickup that pulled up in front is the roach man's and is he going to come waltzing in right now. My mother-in-law is one of them that talks in one sentence forever, without stopping for breath so I don't even have a chance to tell her I am at the kitchen phone trying to cover myself with a pot holder. And I am thinking I should of stayed in that tub. This should be a good lesson. Never answer the phone naked.

You also shouldn't answer it when you are asleep. Say you been up all night with a sick baby, and finally she has dropped off and so have you. Then, of course, the phone rings. And for some reason that got to do with the American work ethic, you know that you can't admit you was asleep in the daytime. So you grope around for the receiver, and you give out with what you think is a real cheerful "Hello-o." But it don't fool the person on the other end of the line. Because they know. They always know. There is this little smug silence and then they say, "Oh. Did I wake you up? Were you *sleeping?*" Now, if anybody deserves to be sleeping it is you. But even if the baby wasn't sick, even if you just laid around all day and polished off a couple cases of bonbons, it still isn't any of their business. But no, you got to make them think you are a hardworking respectable person and you never sleep. So you come up with some lie, like you were cleaning the oven or something else ridiculous.

This never happens to Lout. When he does break down and answer the phone—it don't matter whether it's day or night, or whether he was sleeping or not—

he always does the same thing. He yells, "DO YOU KNOW WHAT TIME IT IS?" He says that gives him the upper hand right away. It sure shakes up the person on the other end of the line. Sometimes they look at their watches and actually tell him what time it is. Real apologetic, too. Like, "Um, well, my watch says it's just three o'clock." But sometimes they don't have a watch and they have to say no, they don't know what time it is and he gets to yell, "IT'S THREE O'CLOCK IN THE AFTERNOON. WHAT DO YOU WANT AT THIS HOUR?" He says his method screens out a lot of undesirables right off the bat—poll-takers, teachers, home room mothers, long-lost relatives, and people in general. About the only person it don't screen out is his mama. Miss Larda just comes right back at him. "Don't ask *me*," she says. "When you going to learn to tell time, boy?"

Miss Larda is always very careful how she answers her phone. She is always worried about getting a ob-scene phone call, so she keeps a whistle next to the receiver. You got to speak up fast when you call her up, because if you don't, she decides it is one of those people that just breathes in the phone and thinks filthy thoughts, and she lets go with a blast that can knock out your eardrums for a week.

A couple weeks ago, she got real upset about one of them calls. And it was my fault. She told me the zipper in one of her favorite slacks gave out, and I told her before she went out and paid for a new one, wait, because I think I had one that might fit. Next day, I remember how I am supposed to measure that zipper and tell her long it is. I am sipping my coffee as I dial the number and just as she picks up, my coffee goes down the wrong way. I hear her saying "Hello? Hello?" and I am trying to answer quick and breathe at the same time and I rasp out, "You want this? It's a good ten inches long." And I hear this shriek and she slams down the phone. A couple minutes later she shows up at my door all out of breath and tells me she got a obscene phone call. What am I going to do? Tell her it was me? They probably got a name for women who make filthy phone calls to their mothers-in-law.

Oh well, at least I wasn't naked when I did it.

# Thank God
# for Indoor Plumbing

I don't know what parents did in the old days before indoor plumbing. I don't mean for the obvious reasons, either. I mean, where did they go to get away from the kids? To me, the bathroom is a whole lot more than a place to wash myself and fix my hair and do other necessary stuff. It is also where I go to look at my *TV Guide* in peace, write down my grocery list, or figure out what is probably going to happen on "All My Children." If the phone rings, somebody else has got to answer it and say we don't want no free estimate on replacing the gutters. Me, I can just spray my rose-garden room deodorizer around, breathe in deep, and think beautiful thoughts. My mother-in-law, Miss Larda, got into the same habit when her kids were coming up, and even though they are all grown now, she says she still goes in there to say her rosary.

But what if I had to go out in the back yard to do this? I don't know if I would take a five-minute hike in the rain to sit and collect my thoughts in a outhouse. Maybe that's why women used to come down with the vapors in those days.

And besides, if we didn't have plumbing inside, what would the kids tell strangers who call up to speak to their mama when you are not home? My kids, if they don't do nothing else right, have got that routine down pat. One Saturday morning I ran down the block to my mother-in-law's, and while I was gone, my son Gargoyle's teacher, Miss Whimp, calls and gets told I am in the bathroom. I come back, and naturally Gargoyle don't mention this call. A little while later, I am taking out the garbage and Miss Whimp calls again and gets told I am still in the bathroom. By this time, she is determined to get ahold of me, and she keeps calling. But every time she does, it happens that my foot is out the door—I go to the TimeSaver grocery; I chase the baby down the block when she trots off with no clothes on; I walk to the mailbox on the corner. And every time, Miss Whimp gets told I am in the bathroom. Anyway, the phone rings around suppertime, and this time I am the one to answer it and it is Miss Whimp and she makes a big deal out of asking me how am I *feeling*. I think that is a odd way to open up a conversation, but all Gargoyle's teachers act funny after a while anyway, so I don't worry about it too much. I don't find out what happened until Gargoyle mentions it when he is going off to bed. And then what am I going to do? Call her back and say,

"Just thought I'd mention that I didn't spend five hours in the bathroom today"? Sometime you just get worse off when you try to explain. But I don't know how I am going to look the woman in the face next

time I have to go to open house. She will probably offer me a bottle of milk of magnesia.

Another time, I tell the two older kids, Gargoyle and my daughter Gumdrop, to watch the baby while I am in the shower. I throw my clothes in the bedroom hamper, I lay my clean ones out on the bed, and I hang the only dry towel in the house, a little one with a picture of Big Bird on it, next to the shower where I can reach it. Like usual, I ignore the notes the kids are shoving under the door. (I should of known God was going to punish me for that. Miss Larda warned me. She herself was in the bathroom the day her daughter eloped. By the time she got around to picking up the note and reading it, Larva was in Mississippi in front of a justice of the peace.)

So I don't read the one which says "Pristine's mother sayed could we go to the show with her so we did. Bye. Gumdrop and Gargoyle." And I don't know I am alone in the house with just Gladiola, who is two years old at the time. I also don't know Gladiola has figured out how to work the bolt on the outside of the bathroom door.

I need to explain this. I named my kids all names that start with G because it goes so nice with Gunch, but what I should of named them was H.T. for Holy Terror. That would of suited them. When Holy Terror I—that's Gumdrop—was little, she had this habit of dropping toothbrushes down the toilet. Holy Terror II, Gargoyle, he had the same taste in fun. So when Holy Terror III came along, I got my husband Lout to put a bolt on the bathroom door—low enough so

Holy Terrors I and II (who by then are not interested in anything to do with toothbrushes) could reach it, but too high for H.T. III.

At least, that's what I think. But this time a light bulb must of gone off on top her head. Because she pushes my bedroom hamper up to the door, and she climbs up on top of it, and she slides that bolt closed from the outside. Now she has got me locked in the bathroom, naked with nothing but a Big Bird towel, and she smirks to her little self and sits down to wait. Pretty soon, she hears the shower stop, and she sees the knob turn, and maybe she even hears me pick up the note. Anyway, after a while I say, soft and sweet, "Gla-adiolaaa?" And she says "What?" And I sort of sing, "Open this door for Mommy, swe-e-etheart," all the time trying not to act panicky and scare her off. "C-a-a-an't," she sings right back. I say it again and she says it again. You got the idea. It goes on and on until she gets tired of it and toddles away, to do whatever she pleases with nobody to stop her. A short fat Frankenstein monster on the loose.

There is one window in the bathroom, and it looks out on an alley. I open it, and I crouch beneath the windowsill, peering over. Luck is with me. I see a man looking underneath the house next door, and I read "Orkin" on the back of his jacket. I flap the towel out the window and call him, and I guess because I was just talking like that to Gladiola, I do it real melodious. "Ro-oach man? Oh, ro-oach man?" He looks up, and from the expression on his face God knows *what* he is thinking. So then I talk fast. I tell him to go get my mother-in-law down the block right now. And he don't say a word. He just walks away. And I am left there to clutch Big Bird and wonder if this roach man is one of them habitual ax murderers and he is gone off to get his ax.

But he isn't, and pretty soon Miss Larda comes huffing and puffing up the alley with my brother-in-law, Leech. Of course, they have to stop under the window and stare at me and shake their heads and say "Mo-dine" and "Tch, tch, I don't believe this" a few times before they waddle around to the front of the house. I hear Leech kicking the front door open and then Miss Larda comes and lets me out. Meanwhile, Gladiola has enjoyed herself. There is a trail of squashed-up food leading up to the TV set, where she is eating a stick of butter.

Well, it could of been a lot worse. She could of locked me in a outhouse. And that is another reason I thank God for indoor plumbing.

# I Ain't Defending
# Litter, but . . .

Most people got a relative like my Aunt Chlorine, and if they don't they should fall down on their knees and give thanks. Aunt Chlorine lives up north (thank God) and she is clean. Very, very clean. She wrote me once that she always spends her Saturday morning scrubbing her "stoop." I am too polite to ask what that is, but it sounds like something I wouldn't write about in a letter if I had to spend all morning scrubbing mine. She probably finishes the job on Saturday afternoon by washing her "buns."

Anyway, I am willing to bet her house is also spotless. For one thing, she is from Montvale, New Jersey. You ever hear of Montvale? It is the home of Lysol. Right off the bat, this tells us her standards are different from us. In New Orleans, we give birth to jazz. In Montvale, they give birth to cleaning fluid.

Around here, we got a different way of looking at life. I ain't defending litter, but you got to admit that it has one advantage. In this town, you learn fast not to walk around daydreaming. You do and God knows what you will step in. Now in Montvale, people probably stroll around on their shiny sidewalks and never once look where they are going. They probably carry around pocket-size copies of Heloise's household hints to read while they walk. And they probably stroll right out in front of a truck. That ain't likely to happen in New Orleans. We learned better the first time we looked up at the sky and stepped on a piece of gum.

Like I said to my mother-in-law, "Trash is in our blood. It's part our culture." What do we do on our biggest holiday? Throw stuff in the street, right? If Mardi Gras is not a orgy for litterbugs, I don't know what it is.

So I am not exactly overjoyed when Aunt Chlorine calls to tell me she is coming to stay with us for a few days. Because she is not going to walk into my house and think it is a lovely sample of our culture. She is going to look at it and think I am scum. Never mind that I work a eight-hour day at the bowling alley. She is not going to blame that mess on Lout and the kids, even though they wallow around in it too. It will be, "That poor man, and those poor children, that lazy woman just never cleans up her house." That's just how her mind works. Sometimes we women are our own worst enemies.

Now, there are three levels of housecleaning, depending on who is coming and how long they are going to be around. Regular cleaning is for, say, when your cousin from Gentilly comes over to bring some mirletons she don't know what to do with. She is going to be in the house for one hour max, and you can make sure she don't get farther than the front room. So you

pitch everything on the floor in that room in a big plastic garbage bag, throw it in the hall locker, and shut the door. You get your husband off the couch and tell him to go put on something decent. And if she can see into the kitchen from where she will sit, you can stick the dirty dishes in the oven. That's about it.

Then there's a in-depth cleaning. That's for when more than one person is coming and they are probably going to wander out the front room. Maybe they will even be around for supper. For this you can't just put stuff in a black plastic bag and throw it in the locker. They might look in there. You got to take it out to the back shed. You got to vacuum the middle of the floor in all the rooms. And either get the dishes out the oven and wash them, or else stick them in the shed and send one of the kids to the TimeSaver for paper plates.

And then there's the biggie—what I call the renovation. Because by the time you are done, the place is so clean it don't look like the same house. (Lout calls it a resurrection. He says stuff resurrects that he ain't seen since we got married.) And I know that is what I am going to have to do for Aunt Chlorine.

At first I don't admit it, though. I tell myself, "Well, who cares what she thinks? She will have to just love us like we are." But I look around at my house, and at the bodies that ain't dead draped across the furniture, and I can see she is not going to love us that way. I am going to have to do something drastic. I am going to set fire to the house. No, I am going to wrap it up in plastic and say we are being fumigated because of snakes. No, I am going to cart in some cans of paint and stepladders and cover everything with dropcloths and tell her the painters are here, don't touch anything.

This is what they call the denial phase. I heard about it on the radio. Next comes the acceptance phase. I face facts. I am going to have to get this house clean.

I mobilize the kids. I tell them I will make them

rich if they do what I say, and if they don't I will sell them on the black market. I put the cat out back with his kitty nibbles and I put my husband Lout out with a six-pack. And we start.

And what we find out is, every time we get through one layer of dirt, we find something else. We pick up the stuff that don't belong on the end table, and underneath is dust. We dust it, and underneath that is scratches that I got to cover up with shoe polish. But we keep at it. We turn the couch cushions to the clean side and put little doilies wherever there are holes. We dab Liquid Paper over the chips on the refrigerator. We sandblast the scum off the bathtub. We wax the no-wax floors with that stuff that really ain't wax that you got to wax no-wax floors with.

Then we are done, and I make the kids promise not to sit down or eat in the house for three days. Aunt Chlorine comes and has her visit and we only have a couple of bad minutes when she tries to stick her slippers under the bed and they won't fit, of course, because of the stuff that is already under there. Finally, she leaves just about the time we are all ready to explode from being nice. We stand on our gleaming front steps and wave bye-bye, and then we go inside and flop down. Lout pops open a beer and the kids slop some Kool-Aid in glasses and I yank out a bottle of Ripple and we all kick off our shoes.

So much for *that* renovation.

# Psychology
# and Trickery

~~~~~~~~~~

My sister-in-law Gloriosa, she keeps going on about how everybody should spend quality time with their kid. Take ten quality minutes every day and plop down and communicate with him. And the rest of the day, that kid can just keep his mouth shut.

But most kids, they want to communicate any old time. Say you go to the swimming pool, and you are sitting there blowing up his "Jaws" inner tube. Right next to you, this lady heaves up over the side, maybe three hundred pounds of her in a hot-pink bathing suit. No way you are going to stop the kid from communicating about *this* sight. Right now. In a voice like a air-raid siren. With his little finger pointing.

You get in a elevator with the kid and he is going to wait until eight or ten other people get on too, and then he is going to look up and communicate that somebody in here got a booger in their nose.

Well, what else can you expect? Kids ain't nothing but little squishy versions of ourselves, and God knows we *want* to say something when this lady rises up out

the pool like a hippopotamus. So you can't expect a kid who ain't had tactfulness pounded into his head yet not to open up his yap.

But when you first have kids, nobody tells you that. You think they are going to work like computers. This is because we are all living in the electric age. We are so used to buying things that got a manual of directions with them, we keep thinking we got to figure out directions to the kids too. We forget we have to treat them just like we treat everybody else. With trickery and threats.

For instance, I remember back when my daughter Gumdrop was little. Gumdrop was a first child and a first grandchild, and she had this wardrobe you wouldn't believe. Little white tights with ruffles on the behind. White shoes. Dresses with little bows and rosettes and ribbons and sashes. Took me forty-five minutes to catch her and shove her into all this just to make a trip to the grocery. Then I would haul her out of her ruffled little car seat and hold her hand and we would walk in the store, all prim and prissy. But sooner or later I would have to turn loose of her hand to reach for something. And what would she do then? She would hit the floor. Every time. Get right down there and start crawling on her belly like a reptile. If there was a slimy spot like where somebody's ice cream had melted, or somebody had dropped some eggs, she'd spot it and slither right through it.

Now if she had been the second or third kid down this would not have bothered me so much because by then you are pretty shell-shocked, and nothing much gets to you anymore. Besides, the clothes would have been broken in by the kid before her. But she was number one and those outfits were brand new.

Anyway, I don't know what to do, so I call up Gloriosa. Gloriosa is the youngest one in my husband Lout's family. Their mama, Miss Larda, she kept this big thick child-care book around and what she used it for, mostly, was for Gloriosa to sit on to eat at the table. Gloriosa decided it was hers and when she got too big to sit on it, she took it to her bedroom. She probably just spread it on her lap for when she polished her nails, but she tells everybody she read it and is now a child psychology expert.

So I tell her about Gumdrop groveling around on the floor. She goes and looks it up. And then she informs me that Gumdrop's daily Grovel Needs are not being met. She says I need to buy her a sandbox and tell her that is her Grovel Area. So I go out and pick out one of them little turtle sandboxes and get my husband Lout to haul in a couple bags of sand. We set it out in the backyard and I dress Gumdrop in her sun-and-surf rompers and bring her outside and tell her to go to it. She looks at that sandbox and then she looks at me. Then she tells me that the sandbox is full of dote. I figure she means dirt, and so I sit down and I communicate with her about clean dote, which is sand, and dotey dote, which is what comes out of the ashtrays she likes to turn over. I don't have no luck, which ain't surprising, since I sound like a fool even to me.

Finally one day my mother-in-law happens to be at the grocery with me and Gumdrop. Here we are waiting in the checkout line and Gumdrop, in her little pink sunsuit with forty-two ruffles across her buns, gets loose and snakes under the candy display. Miss Larda, who has a voice that carries for a couple miles in any direction, she just leans over and says, "Gumdrop, precious heart, WATCH OUT FOR THEM ROACHES!"

Well, like magic, that child pops right out from

under that counter. Right out, and stands up straight like a little lady. A lot of other people who had been kind of slouching in the line pop up straight too, and start glaring around at the floor. Now that's communication. And my mother-in-law didn't even take no course in it.

(I never saw no roaches, and I think the manager was coming over to communicate with us about that, but we was just leaving.)

Anyway, Miss Larda probably could use that method to get herself to the front of a line waiting for a table at a restaurant too. Or up to the front row of the auditorium for Gumdrop's dance review. Or for anything she wants. But I don't think I am going to mention it. You got to be careful how you use real potent weapons.

# A Pot for Every Chick

Around this city, we got a delicate problem, and people don't talk about it too much. But I bet you if I ran for mayor I would talk about it, and I would win too.

It's about Mardi Gras. Think about it. What makes the difference, for you personally, between a good Mardi Gras and one that is a disaster? Now, some people say their daughter has got to be queen of some Carnival krewe or something. And other people got to be in the French Quarter all got up in a costume made out of a million sequins and three feathers; or else they got to go down there and *stare* at somebody dressed like that.

But that ain't what you really *need*. Think basic.

You get up in the morning on Carnival Day, and maybe you pack a thermos with coffee and you bring along a couple six-packs of beer and some soft drinks. And you go downtown, and you drink the coffee and you break out the other stuff and start sipping. And after a while what do you need? I don't got to tell you what you need. But there probably isn't any around. So you walk and walk and walk and finally you find one and there are twenty drunks lined up in front of it.

You can't tell me no different. What you need more than anything else is a nice comfort station.

For me it ain't so bad. My husband, Lout, and his brothers, Leech and Lurch, they pop open one beer after the other and every once in a while one of them says "Excuse me" and walks off and it don't take no genius to know he just went a few blocks to where nobody was looking and stepped behind a big bush. And he comes back with this relieved look on his face. And me and my mother-in-law, Miss Larda, and my daughter Gumdrop are all hopping from one foot to the other because we don't want to go wait in line twenty minutes to get into a place where you got to hold your breath the whole time.

It ain't fair. And if women had been in charge of this city and Mardi Gras for the last hundred years, we would have solved that problem by now. If I was running for mayor, my slogan would be, "A commode on every corner." Lout says it ought to be, "A pot for every chick." Very funny. This is serious business.

They probably have the same problem at that Rose Bowl Parade in Pasadena, and at the Macy's

Thanksgiving Day Parade, and just about any other parade anywhere. Of course, on Mardi Gras you are out all day long and into the night. So their problems probably ain't even a drop in the bucket compared to ours. I mean it.

Of course, if I was to run for office, I would have to do it under a made-up name. I am not about to go down in history as Modine Gunch, the mayor who brought more toilets to Mardi Gras. They'd probably name them after me, and call them Gunch-lets or something disgusting like that.

Maybe that's why none of the other mayors have done it.

Or it could be because those other mayors are men. Don't get me wrong. I got nothing against men. But you got to admit they have got a talent for not seeing what is right under their nose, and toilets is just one example.

Take Lout, for instance. A few years ago, he decides what he needs is a pickup truck. It don't matter that he never hauls anything bigger than his bowling ball. Real men drive pickup trucks, with big tall tires and rifle racks. And Lout's friend Railbird has one he has to get rid of at a sacrifice because he is supposedly moving overseas or somewheres, so he comes over to take us for a ride. I climb in and I naturally slide over to make room for Lout. I don't realize that there is a stick shift coming out of the floor, and I am sitting with one knee on either side of it. So when Railbird reaches over to shift gears, I let out this little ladylike squeal and sort of leap over into Lout's lap. Lout, being as he don't notice the obvious, bugs out his eyes like I have gone right out of my mind, but he just clears his throat and keeps talking man talk with Railbird.

Anyway, two days later he actually buys this truck. I can't understand this. Why does anybody want

to get something that makes you spend half the time shoving back and forth on a gear shift and stomping down on a clutch, and punishes you when you make a mistake by screeching its gears, when you can get one that just purrs along and minds its own business while you mind yours? Obviously, this is a truck for people who like to torture theirselves. It is like buying 100 percent cotton handwashable clothes now that permanent press has been invented. These manufacturers have spent years and years inventing stuff to make life easier and what do we do? We got to prove we're tough. Iron them shirts. Shift them gears. Next thing we will all be disconnecting our showers and saying how invigorating it is to bathe in a tin tub in front the stove.

Anyway, back to Mardi Gras. Come to find out, Railbird is a member of the Krewe of Bacchus. And as a perk for buying the truck, he sends tickets for me and Lout and Miss Larda and Gumdrop to the big bash they throw after the Bacchus parade. And as far as I am concerned, that makes up for the truck. Lout can drive around on a tractor if he wants to, if I get to go to the Bacchus Rendezvous.

Railbird asks Lout to get there a couple hours early to help out. So on the big night, Lout leaves while I am still getting ready. I put on my new long strapless and my high-heeled gold sandals with ties that wrap around my legs. Miss Larda has squished herself into her black formal. It is one of those kind that tends to slide down the front, so she has stuck a Mardi Gras corsage in her cleavage to preserve her modesty. Gumdrop is balancing on the highest heels she ever wore in her life, and she got her hair all kinked and moussed stiff and she is afraid to move her head. We all tell each other how gorgeous we look, and we mince out the door.

And then we get the shock of our lives. Lout has driven off in my car and left us the pickup.

I start to say just what I think of Lout, but my mother-in-law tells me I should be thankful he left me a nice big safe truck to drive. So we hike up our long skirts and haul ourselves in. Ever see one of those movies where the pilot plops over stone dead and the other person in the plane has to take over flying it? This is what driving this truck is like. I am trying to remember the little bit I noticed from when I rode in it with Railbird, and I get it started up and off we go snorting and bucking to the ball. Miss Larda starts up with "Hail Mary, full of grace" and Gumdrop is whining, "God, Ma, turn on the radio," and I am so nervous I don't know whether to spit or go blind. And we don't even know yet that Lout also left a sack of his crab bait—which happens to be day-old chicken necks—in the back.

We know it once we open the windows though. And when we get downtown and go to pull in the parking garage, the man in the ticket booth is pretty emphatic about waving us away. Then he comes out the booth looking like he is gagging, but I think that is just a act. Anyway, we chug around a while and we wind up parking way over by some railroad tracks. And there is nothing else to do but get out and walk back along the tracks in our high heels, keeping a eye out for rapists and murderers and every once in a while stepping in the mud. The only good thing about it is listening to Miss Larda. Now her voice is music to my ears. She is saying "Divorce him, Modine! God will understand."

But what would I do then? Marry another man, who would do the exact same kind of thing? They are all alike.

Maybe I just as soon make up a name and run for mayor.